WHERE'S THE OFFICE?

MOVING TODAY'S LEADERS FROM WHAT **IS** TO WHAT **CAN BE**

WILFORD A. LEWIS
&
HEATHER HANSEN O'NEILL

authorHOUSE®

AuthorHouse™
1663 Liberty Drive
Bloomington, IN 47403
www.authorhouse.com
Phone: 833-262-8899

Published by AuthorHouse 11/02/2021

ISBN: 978-1-6655-4175-6 (sc)
ISBN: 978-1-6655-4174-9 (e)

Library of Congress Control Number: 2021921474

Print information available on the last page.

There have been so many people in our lives who have contributed to this book. From those who provided support, editing, research, and tech assistance to those who have offered wisdom, guidance and inspiration.

To the focus groups and industry experts who ensured the content relevance in today's world. Whether assistance with overarching themes, validation, specific quotes, or those who preferred to remain anonymous.

From The Phoenix community to the Lights of the Roundtable. From family to friends. Those who provided a caring ear and idea bouncing. Or even a suggestion or two we may not have wanted (but needed) to hear. All brought value and are greatly appreciated!

Whether you inspired us with your vision and ideas from afar, or touched us with your kindness every single day, we thank you.

Karin Williams	Dr. Eben Alexander	Peg Thoms
Ed Farmer	Karen Newell	Jesse Farmer
Katie Sprock	Dawn Penfold	Mitch Rothschild
Kelly Williams	Peggy Bud	Bonnie Marcus
Jake, Luke, and Liam	Matt Bartelme	Jan Sopata
O'Neill	Shing Wong	Missy Bohn
Sue Alexander	Tracy Judge	Jamie Lynn
Lesa Hiben	Alan Ibbotson	Daniela Fazoli
Robert Lauterborn	Melody Garcia	Bart Berkey
Michael Dominguez	Katina Athanasiou	David Reiderman
Todd Cherches	Luisa Ferrario	Bryan Mattimore
Cheryl Brzezinski	Sterena Strickland	Sandra Long
Claudine Maidique	Michael Burke	Jamie Williams

We have great gratitude for the leaders who made us and great hope for the leaders we seek to encourage with our words here. We have faith that you can move beyond what is and create a greater version of what can be.

CONTENTS

FOREWORD

Outstanding leadership has never been a harder objective to achieve than in today's rapidly changing environment. Whether we consider the advance of our technology adoption curve, the multi-generational influences within those we serve (team members and clients), or the ever-changing geopolitical instability – the world has become not only fast paced, but quite complex. Throw in a global pandemic and you understand that how you led last year, last week, or even yesterday is simply not good enough.

I have often told those leaders I serve that "Leadership is a muscle and like all muscles it must be nourished and exercised to be strong." It is a journey that will not and should not ever end, and the goal is unattainable. Thus, the work never stops.

When my good friend Heather Hansen O'Neill asked me to write this foreword for "Where's the Office," I couldn't have been more honored nor excited. To understand that together with Will Lewis, they took the opportunity to write a book that could be hugely impactful to all leaders, as it is such a great pause and reflection of the many situational changes, we are dealing with in the world today.

Unlike anytime in recent history, there is such a need for strong leader development, as the dynamic complexity will continue to move at a very rapid pace. To help leaders understand the mobility of leadership and the need to remain agile in our approach is different than the hierarchical leadership that was customary for many decades.

The understanding of people and our own emotions (emotional intelligence) is lacking in many leadership roles, as those leaders are traditionally strategically brilliant and own strong intellectual capacity. What is found often is those talents that helped build these important skills are different than the understanding and need of emotional development. Great communication will never be achieved without great understanding.

Heather and Will have tackled not only these important issues, but they have given us a template to make many of these important concepts actionable. As leadership is all about service, they have served all of us well by not only teaching, but rather showing each of us how we can work our leadership muscle. I for one am thankful to both for allowing me to exercise!

~Michael Dominguez, President & CEO,
Associated Luxury Hotels International

INTRODUCTION

We're now living in a world of the "4 Any's" wherein—when it comes to knowledge workers—pretty much Anyone can do Anything at Anytime from Anywhere. For, as the pandemic era has demonstrated, people can be just as productive (if not more so) working from home as when they were working in an office, and that where you do your work and when you do your work no longer matters.

So, in answer to the question, "Where's the office?" the answer is: It's wherever you are.

Back in the day, young, ambitious employees would excitedly accept an entry level job in the mailroom, with aspirations of someday—many years from now—working their way up the career ladder to the proverbial corner office. But there are no more mailrooms—because there is no more mail (and there is no "email room," as far as I know). And if you want a "corner office," you don't have to wait 30 years; you can have one right now, simply by setting up a nice comfortable desk in a corner of your home or by finding a cozy corner table at your local Starbucks.

However, in this new hybrid world of work, while some things have changed forever, certain aspects remain the same. Leadership is still important—in fact, it is more important than ever. As are an organization's mission, vision, values, and culture. And effective communication is absolutely crucial. For me, personally, all of my "visual leadership" work involves getting others to "see" what we're saying… as well as "flipping the eye" so as to be able to see the world through the lens of others—with empathy and compassion—with the goal of helping them to turn their visions into realities.

Which brings me to Heather Hansen O'Neill and Will Lewis.

There's a classic saying (origin unknown) that "The best leaders don't light a fire under people… they light a fire within them." And that's what Heather does for a living… and does so well. Not only does she light up a room and light up a stage just through her presence, but via her "From Fear to Fire" works, she ignites personal transformation through her training, coaching, speaking, and teaching. The poet William Butler Yeats wrote that "Education is not the filling of a pail, but the lighting of a fire"—and Heather exemplifies this principle in everything she does. So, now, as people try to figure out who they are and where they fit in this new world of work, her sparks of enlightenment and inspiration are needed now more than ever.

Which brings me to Will Lewis. About a year ago, Heather contacted me and said, "There's this guy I'd like you to meet, and who'd like to meet you. He's amazing. You're going to love meeting him. Trust me. Oh, and by the way, he's 91."

Trusting Heather's judgment implicitly, I drove a half hour through long and winding, unfamiliar Connecticut country roads to meet Will at his home, with Heather there, on the enclosed porch of what looked like a rustic inn atop a rolling hilltop featuring a stable of horses. Where the heck am I, and what am I doing here? I asked myself as I knocked on the screen door and let myself in. Long story short… Heather was right, and it was a meeting I will never forget… although in some ways, looking back, it was a blur as we covered so much ground in such a brief period of time.

Ninety-one years young, Will energetically and enthusiastically walked me through his career background and his visionary innovations that were years ahead of their time. In fact, his presentation even featured printed handouts of some of his work (!), as well as insightful questions and comments about mine.

So, Heather was right, I sat there thinking to myself: This guy is amazing. He is brilliant. He is a visionary. He is a force. He is…

"Will Power"! And, as the saying goes: "Where there's a 'Will,' there's a way."

So, when it comes to the future of work, I am glad that we have Will—and Heather—to show us the way, to lead the way, and to help us get from what is to what can be.

~Todd Cherches, CEO of BigBlueGumball and author of *VisuaLeadership: Leveraging the Power of Visual Thinking in Leadership and in Life*

PREFACE

Sitting in 'Nature's Cathedral,' aka Will Lewis' beautiful backyard, you wouldn't know that two days ago a tornado had blown through. Nor would you suspect that this well-spoken friend of mine was 91. Certainly there was nothing telling in the insightful conversation. Nor in the recent medical update that his doctor advised only an increase in Vitamin D. "That's it?!" Yes, that's it.

On this day, Will's excitement and insistence that we work together to share his work stood out. This showed a desire to leave a legacy. And I cannot express the honor I feel or the enormity of the gift he has given, not just to me but also to the world.

Will has had an illustrious career that has taken him from the Navy to GE, to building a school for underserved women in the 60's, to conducting trainings on mindset and leadership for the FBI, the CIA, and more.

At the time of this writing, he was teaching wood working to senior citizens (20 years his junior!), working with me, lunching often with a plethora of friends, and reading... a lot. Every time we met, Will would share a new relevant book on consciousness or artificial intelligence or our global economy. His insatiable need to stimulate his brain is obvious as he makes his way through book after book from the library. The topics may be varied but his quest for ongoing development is unending.

This need to expand the boundaries of his mind was what led to our meeting many years ago. It's really a great story.

In 2014, I (Heather Hansen O'Neill) was conducting an evening program called Ignite Your Income at the local library for SCORE (Service Corps of Retired Executives). My program helped entrepreneurs understand their style and strengths and use them to enhance relationships to grow their business. Toward the end of the event Will stepped outside because what I said led him to want to show me something he had in his car. Unfortunately, the door locked behind him and Will is far too considerate to want to interrupt the meeting by knocking to be let in. So, he went home.

I was afraid he left because he didn't like it!

The next day he emailed me to say that he enjoyed the session, had a few more questions, and wanted to know if I could meet for lunch to discuss them. We did, and after a lovely two-hour meal, where I learned much of his adventures and fascinating business career, he took out his checkbook.

I was beyond shocked, "What's that for?!" He wanted to join a coaching program I was starting because he was fired up about his new business idea. I was deeply impressed by both his vast experience and his desire to always be learning, growing, and contributing. My experience was more with people who gave up when things became difficult. Or who were so stuck thinking of things the same way all the time they couldn't even consider new perspectives.

Will has always been both a breath of fresh air and a wealth of knowledge. Every time we meet, I walk away with a new idea, an interesting resource, or seeing the world in a brand-new way. We have become good friends.

Several of the concepts and stories that Will has shared struck me as being explicitly pertinent to what is going on in our current world. Specifically Will's thoughts about change, progress, and the necessity of moving from physical space to mind space. These notions aren't just theory. They are tools and guidelines that can help bring peace, clarity, confidence, and leadership to our current chaos.

He envisioned them over 50 years ago. He is a visionary and passionate about sharing the message with leaders looking to make a real difference in the world. The earth-shattering events of our current time made Will's message all the more important. A book was calling out to be written. Now was the time.

At the writing of this manuscript, we're digging our way out of the COVID-19 pandemic. The world is in a state of great flux, fear, and change. We will dive into how this motivated the timeliness of the writing of the book; however, you may be reading this at some future date.

Don't let the fact that our current situation is now in your past lead you to think that this book's concepts are any less valid. We have reached a tipping point. We can no longer go back to stagnancy and consistency to the degree to which we've been accustomed.

These ideas Will foresaw have been revitalized and combined with relevant new success stories. Extensive research, focus groups, and surveys have been conducted to further validate that the concepts and tools are not only applicable for leaders today, but cutting edge. They can help you release inertia and embrace a new perspective with transformational leadership potential.

I have great faith that no matter when you are reading this book that you are in a state of change. The only certainty is that life will forevermore be uncertain. And our ability to adapt to change and to take back control of our mindset, choices, and behaviors is our greatest asset.

We tell our stories throughout the book to illustrate the takeaway. Sometimes the story is mine and sometimes it is from Will.

It's not about a story you read here but about the idea it sparks for you. You'll want to connect the concepts to lessons you've already learned. Allow it to seep into you and inspire new perspectives and innovative solutions.

Remember—this is your journey. Take what you can use, leave what doesn't fit. Take action on what speaks to you and recognize that the power lies within you to move from what is to what can be.

Quiet the external noise around you so you can turn up the volume on your heart, your intuition, your connection to meaning. We believe that incredible leadership happens when people pay less attention to career and more to whole life, when every single day is seen as a rare, precious gift. Remind yourself that today is not a rehearsal—this is your life. And you have within you the capability to make a real and lasting difference.

This book was never meant to be stagnant, to be kept upon your shelf. It longs to be read, dog-eared, highlighted, and acted upon. Its mission is to stoke an inner fire, to show you that you already have within you everything you need, and to light a pathway forward to a greater purpose and ever evolving leadership potential.

Because that's what the world needs right now. It needs leaders who think deeper, who make connections, who take both responsibility and action.

Enjoy!

"Cocreation is more than collaboration. When cocreation occurs individuals bring all that each can offer to a joint effort and, at the same time, open themselves to a larger, or higher, idea that may not previously occurred to either of them."
From Seat of the Soul by Gary Zukav

We are grateful that cocreation such as this has catapulted *Where's the Office?* beyond either of us.

CHAPTER 1

WHERE'S THE OFFICE?

Section 1: What and where is it?

Here we look at the transition 'the office' is making in the world and how we use it as an analogy to provide new, better ways of leading.

The office isn't what it used to be. We can't hold fast to what it was, because we'll miss out on what it could be.

"A room, set of rooms, or building used as a place for commercial, professional, or bureaucratic work" is how we've seen and used 'office' for so long. But the world has forced our hand in defining a space for growth and leadership that expands beyond the four walls of a traditional office... and this is a gift.

During the COVID-19 pandemic, protocol was to send non-essential workers into a remote work environment. People were told to set up shop in their homes to stay safe and make it through the crisis. They were forced to figure out how to remain productive while dealing with smaller spaces that may be occupied with other family members with their own 'office' needs or other priorities. Families needed to navigate all of this while also home-schooling children. It was, in many cases, chaos.

Some were unaccustomed to being disciplined enough to work with the extra distractions. Some didn't have those distractions; those living and working alone felt isolated and lonely. Above all, the uncertainty and fear people experienced couldn't be ignored. It's difficult to thrive when you can't see the light at the end of the tunnel. When you can't see an end in sight.

Humans are resilient creatures. More so than we even realize. We learned to adapt. We figured it out. We made do, and some even flourished.

The office isn't what it used to be. It doesn't look the same, it doesn't feel the same, and we cannot treat it the same. When companies started to say, "It's time to come back to the office" employees started to say, "Maybe I don't want to." There were benefits of this new work/life balance. Independence, flexibility, ease. There were benefits to returning to the office. Connection, collaboration, communication. The employees wanted a say. They wanted the freedom to choose.

Webster Dictionary offers an alternate definition of office as "a service done for another." It's one of our favorites from the standpoint that it doesn't fit into a physical space but instead is in your mind and your actions, with a focus on how well you serve.

In leading forward we cannot underestimate the importance of service. How we lead others influences their ability to adapt, transition, and make their own impact. Our individual actions make an impression on our teams, our clients, and, ultimately, the viability of our companies.

What's possible when we engage ourselves in the difficult but rewarding practice of conceptualization? What's possible when delegation of influence, authority, responsibility, and reward are seen as pointless as the sun saying to the earth, "You're on your own"? Anyone approaching our solar system from a distance would know that in many respects—radiation, warmth, light, gravitational influence—the earth is well inside the sun. Our people are in our orbit just as the earth is within the sun's. Acting as the type of leader who guides, communicates, and trusts will shine a light on the uniqueness of who they are and what they are capable of.

What's possible when leaders recognize that all who look to them for leadership can be empowered—and must be empowered, for effectiveness and self-esteem.

This change in perception, as well as the reality of our world, is at the core of the most important takeaways you'll find here.

- We are not tied to old ways.
- Things are changing and that is positive.
- Top leaders can release their resistance and expand their minds to make the most of these changes.
- Doing so opens up opportunities to make a significant difference in their people, their companies, and the world.

Today's office isn't a location but is, instead, a mindset

Think about it. People are no longer tied to a physical office space. Why remain tied to the systems, processes, and mindsets that are rooted in that physical limitation? Moving forward requires new ways of looking at people, business, and the world. It opens our options, stimulates innovative solutions, and provides new ways of networking and collaboration.

Companies need to look at many things, including the type of work they do, the need for in-person teamwork, the cost effectiveness of remote work, and many other factors, as well as the desire of their employees. Leaders need to combine big picture vision with customized, individual solutions. And they require a new way of communicating, a new way of thinking that ensures effective leadership in any scenario. You, as one of today's leaders, need to think and behave differently to optimize your situation, your team, your company, your community, and your mind.

As with most change, you may resist at first. Allow for that resistance. Breathe into it. The uncertainty will pass faster that way.

When you push past your comfort zone into this new way of leading, it has the power to transform your life. You elevate your connection to self, to team, to purpose, and meaning. Not only do you become a better example for your team, but you also access a deeper connection to a greater energy.

You find a new awareness and ways of communicating that increase your relationship with your team and with your own intuition and intention. This is where the top leaders reside, where time and focus are in flow, and where you align with your purpose in a way that the universe conspires to help you achieve it.

Communication from this space is more inclusive and effective. We've seen companies experience massive morale issues because leadership didn't push past their discomfort and communicate during difficult times. The ones who were able to do so created a safe environment for expression of all the emotions that accompany change. Only when we give space for this process can our people release the negativity and move forward to understanding how the change will benefit them.

Open the lines of communication

Allow and encourage emotion, pushback, idea storming, and more. These tactics of expanding rather than controlling will help your team not only while working remotely, but also in all areas of their collaboration. The expansion is good for the health of the employees and is especially beneficial for the health of your business. You will need it as teams work more remotely, because when you don't, they suffer.

One of our base needs is security. Ongoing change leaves people feeling less secure than they expected with their careers. Imagine the engagement of minds when security as we have known it changes. What organization today can guarantee lifetime security for anyone? What evidence is there today that even marriage can afford lifetime security?

What if there was a new security, where at its foundation was mental and physical health? Many people cling to jobs that seriously erode both mental and physical health. At the next level of the new security is growth—essential for maintaining economic and mental well-being—and transcendence; a state often experienced but rarely sustained. What happens when the numbing state of the old and false security is compared with this new, real security?

When you share the concepts you find here with your team, you'll increase morale, overall productivity, and achieve higher levels of service. This 'service done for another' is your new 'office.' It's not about where you are but how you are; how you show up. You carry it with you.

Leading change may feel uncomfortable. Any pattern or habit adaptation begins that way. Take consistent actions toward the change. Come back to the tools you'll learn here regularly. This consistency will bring a new level of comfort—a levelling up of your skills. This will be reinforced when you witness the outcome of growth and making a real difference.

One element of our changing times is personalization. You have more choices. Marketing experts are all about "personalization"—software designers talk about "customizing the user experience." Give yourself the same wisdom as you consider the future. Make deeply personal the journey you embark on and customize the value you take away from the experience of change. It may not be as easy as following the crowd and working in status quo; however, leading change is far more rewarding. To practice here focus on personalizing this journey—the journey of growth you experience from the lessons held in this book.

Discover what works for your company. Work through the exercises and see how the ideas fit for you and your team. Make active decisions by considering where you are and where you want to go—examine the gap. You will know which concepts will add the most value and will build the bridge. When you do, you expand beyond leading a company into leading your life and showing the same possibilities to your team.

Our new, more portable office is not what we imagined. What we thought was a temporary and necessary conversion to virtual work has lasted longer than we ever expected. For some it has shown increased efficiency and a more satisfying quality of life. Learning how to maximize remote work has become a focus for these companies. Depending on the company and the industry, other businesses are clamoring to return to in person meeting, to reestablish those deeper ties. There is no one size fits all mentality. *Today's office isn't a location but instead a mindset.*

As you read further, our stories will span time and space and you'll see that nothing we discuss relates directly to a big office building or even an office in your home. It relates to the office WITHIN you. The office of the mind. One that sets your spirit free to innovate. The one to which you can 100% own, take responsibility for, and use to expand productivity, unleash creativity, and enjoy solution-focused results. The one where your inner leader can chart a new course, for management isn't what it was. You get to choose.

When we realize that 'the office' resides within us, we foster self-leadership in our people to take responsibility for their productivity, their mindset, and their performance. We understand the power of sharing an inspired vision that can light the way for them.

We are moving from what IS to what CAN BE.

Section 2: Why is it?

> *Here we look at why this new concept of an office can benefit you as a leader personally as well as why your team, company, and community will find value.*

Why? We have a vision. A vision to provide leaders with a common language, a greater purpose, and the inspiration to spark meaningful change. A new wave of leadership that works from the inside out and lights the path for their team members to work at peak performance wherever they are, wherever their office may be.

Why? Because YOU can influence change. We believe that leaders of the future are the ones who impact the people who impact people.

What's possible when we learn more about the mind and how to engage it? What's possible when we learn how to create an environment for the mind? And what's possible when we combine human aspirations with our work?

When we learn more about the mind and how to engage it, we will gain new and profound respect for ourselves and others. We will connect without regard to age, sex, race, religion, education, or nationality but rather as humans having a human experience. That each of us have value and our diverse experiences and perspectives are required to create a harmony of meaning, purpose, and possibility.

Thought for the day:

"My friend has a circular driveway, and he can't get out..."

There is a circle of life, and we know and appreciate the infinite energy and possibility within it.

However, we've found that potential leaders can get stuck in the cycle of uncertainty. They repeat patterns that aren't serving them based on beliefs that may not even be theirs. This rotation of unhelpful habits and ways of thinking keep people from moving forward, from innovating, from becoming their best selves. They get stuck.

We've created a way for leaders to communicate that transcends time and space. A movement into Mind SPACE, using the Seven Levels of Communication to inspire top managers to rise to greater heights of personal and professional leadership. Our focus on understanding where you are and where you want to go with Mind SPACE and the Seven Levels of Communication (which you're about to be introduced to) is all about movement. Here is where the energy within the circle can be released, used, and expanded. Movement generates energy that magnifies action and opportunity.

We know that dance has the power to generate energy and release obstacles. Choreographing dances enables you to work through problems using your body. Every turn, sway, jump, or step can unleash an inner force of creative spirit that enables you to see solutions that otherwise were blocked.

Many leaders release these blocks with walking meetings, stretching, breath work, a run, kayak, or other joyful activities.

Our kitchen appliances when unplugged are of little use. When plugged in their potential increases. When actually turned on, you have actioned that potential.

Electricity is still there when the appliance is turned off or unplugged, but is not being utilized. When we remain in that state of being 'stuck' in the cycle of bad habits or trapped in uncertainty, our brains are like unused electricity. It's our potential. But until we spark movement with conscious thought and action it's not being fully utilized. Movement is like plugging in your brain to the electrical current!

If you feel mentally or emotionally exhausted, an effective starting point through it is to change your physical state. A brisk walk, rolling your shoulders, or even moving to a new room can spark a shift. When you're stuck in your head, move your body. Some days the release will come faster, others it will take time. But you'll know when it happens. There's a shift in your breathing, a liberation of energy. You'll let go of the stress enough to be able to at least contemplate new viewpoints, ideas, options, and solutions. Only when this happens will you be able to come back to your mind in the right state.

As leaders, recognizing this relationship between energy and innovation is the first step. Creating the personal habit of it to lead by example is the second. And sharing this strategy and even incorporating it into meetings is the final step.

Recognize that development and progress come from consciously choosing new patterns. Patterns of both thought and behavior. You can create new patterns to release stuck energy through moving your body (body to mind). AND you can come at it from conscious choice to let go of the old habit of worry, regret, and fear (mind to body). Then, through consistent thought and action, you create a new, more effective habit.

In the same vein, you have the power to examine and pick the beliefs that serve you and release the ones that don't. Understand your mindset and where it stems from. That openness leads to an increased awareness and ability to develop new responses to the world as well as decisive activities that can bring about new results. **Results of Your Choosing.**

If every morning you wake up and you say this is not a rehearsal, this is real, then you can do something about it. A service for another. Take action to make a difference. This is how real change occurs. Like Gail Lowney Alofsin, professor and author of *Your Someday is NOW—What Are You Waiting For?* said in her interview on the From Fear to Fire podcast, "Live with undeniable joy because this is not our practice life." How does this apply in business leadership?

This is your career. Your team. Your clients. Your results. Your impact. You must DO something. Take action.

When you own your choices and establish best practices and habits, then amazing opportunities arise. We tend to say "the universe is conspiring for us to..."

There was serendipity in the timing and purpose of how we met and the idea for this book came to be. It crossed beyond circumstance to deep significance time and time again. We realized with conviction that we needed to 'do something about it.' The meaning was bigger than us. It catapulted us to action. To the writing of this book.

There are synchronous circumstances that occur for you too, should you choose to become aware of them. Thinking of a friend several times, then they call. Getting stuck in traffic then realizing that the delay saved you from something else. Missing that promotion you thought you wanted, then getting a bigger, better one you would have missed had you gotten the first one. These things happen all day long. When we notice and act on them, there is unlimited potential to make a difference.

What can be and what's possible become bigger than you, and that's where purpose comes in... That's when we feel compelled to do something. To do something beyond the complacency of what people are feeling right now.

People are experiencing great challenge. And during difficulty it can be hard to see the beauty and the lessons all around us. During challenge, people often see the negative more and then make it bigger with their focus.

But there is good all around us. Prospects, openings, solutions, connections, and options. Choose to concentrate on the positive energy and opportunity. That attention will contribute to its expansion.

What inspires YOU?

"We shall not cease from exploration, and the end
of all our exploring will be to arrive where we
started and know the place for the first time."
~T.S. Eliot

What's possible in your business? In your life?

Consistency of Change

"When you become comfortable with uncertainty,
infinite possibilities open up in your life."
~Eckhart Tolle

The Enchanted Loom by Robert Jastrow traces the evolution of the human mind from the little shrew behind the trees in the age of the dinosaur into present day. It recaps the early history of life then focuses on intelligence and the evolution of the brain. Within it lies the concept "Flexible behavior is the essence of intelligence."

We are always evolving. Your mission as a part of the human race, should you choose to accept it, is to evolve. Use the ideas you receive here, in some way, to change your mind, your perspective, or your behavior. Change, not for the sake of change but as part of your own evolutionary process, unleashes the potential within you. The ability to adapt and advance is the most powerful leadership skill you can build.

A leader in the world of entrepreneurial ventures and most recently Chairman of Vitals Mitch Rothschild said, "One of the rules of evolution is not the strongest or the fastest or the smartest survive, it's the ones who are most adaptable to change. I'm an entrepreneur, so I felt for the longest time that the shortest distance between two places might be a zigzag."

He continues, "We don't just get from here to there easily. We go to school and our brains are trained to believe we can think our way through everything. But that's not really how it works. You have to somewhat plan but it's as much or more about coming up with an overview and figuring out the next three moves."

If we as leaders can learn to be forward focused, to be agile in our pursuit of goals, our teams and companies reflect that as well, creating new opportunity, new benefit, and future relevance. And in so doing, we more capably define what that future looks like. We know where we go and are open to different paths on how to get there.

We've been operating our businesses and managing our workforce for decades according to theories and assumptions that are no longer optimal. The ideas that have worked in the past need to adapt. If our assumptions are based solely on what was once true, we lose the opportunity to move forward more freely, tied to a past that is no longer relevant. We cannot make assumptions based on facts that are no longer facts. We must be present in the moment and adapting on the daily.

What's possible when we develop and employ a new language which suits our needs and helps us engage our brains? Why carry on with words like productivity when creative synthesis is obviously more powerful and accurate? Why limit our accounting to the accounting system which accounts for bricks, mortar, cash, and capital equipment and does not account for the value of a single "enchanted loom," to say nothing of many engaged and powered by a shared vision?

Resilience and Adaptability

Our current crisis is less an overwhelming challenge than it is a massive opportunity to become better.

An opportunity to shift, to make change, to move from where you are to where you want to be. To plot out what's needed to create new systems, new ways to assess, new ways of communicating. Using the tools of Mind SPACE and the Seven Levels of Communication, you'll be able to produce more results and greater impact.

So often we stay in one place doing a specific activity or process because we are comfortable. When things are okay, humans don't change. When we are comfortable, we stay. We hold tight to an attachment to what we know, no matter how mundane or ineffective that might be. You may even hear, "We have always done it that way" without asking why or if it is as effective as it once might have been.

The act of becoming uncomfortable, whether we choose it, or it is thrust upon us, is a primary motivator to take the actions that lead to better outcomes. This external force can either constrain or compel a reaction. The pandemic is just one example.

We have worked with many people caught up in the vicious cycle of resistance. "Why me?" and "How could this happen?" turns the focus to external blame. This gives up our power and produces a feeling of being stuck.

Even when things outside of our control occur, we as leaders can take responsibility for how we lead, what we think, and what we do with it. Consistently taking ownership of our responses to external forces generates the patterns of responsibility and plants the seeds of resilience. Resilience is about being able to withstand or recover quickly from difficult situations. This pattern of ownership of your responses is an important strategy for increasing agile mindset and behavior.

"Resilience and adaptability are the lessons we're learning. These lessons can be applied to running a business more efficiently in this new environment." Bonnie Marcus, author of *The Politics of Promotion* and *Not Done Yet*! contributed.

Hospitality professional David Riederman says, "We don't know what tomorrow brings. Perhaps we thought we did but we truly don't. We're either a victim or a volunteer of circumstance. When you transition out of something that you've been very familiar with to something that you're not familiar with, it's important to acknowledge it. In doing so, you'll uncover that the other person you're communicating with may be just as uncomfortable. It's been pretty amazing the last six months in finding the silver linings. I find them every day."

Section 3: Who is it?

*Here we come fully into the office being within you
and how you'll want to customize this process to work
best for you.*

YOU are the office. It is within you. Whether you are leading the collaboration of a small team of engineers in the conference room or conducting a sales conference at a large venue. Whether you are virtually overseeing 100 global marketing reps or sitting on the beach envisioning new ways to engage your clients. When you show up as your best self, being able to assess the various needs of your people, in any scenario, in any location, you are the future of leadership fully utilizing the power of your creative mind.

There are instances of it all around us. Watch, for example, the widening of the pupils of a small child's eyes when a chocolate chip cookie appears. Watch the arms and legs flail away until the prize is in the mouth.

Imagine leaders determined to engage minds with eye-popping presentations and encounters. Imagine what happens when executives admit that dreams, visions, and concepts cannot be contained within the limits of one neatly typed page. Imagine leaders who insist that market data does not create markets. That, in fact, markets are people, real live human beings, making decisions, day in and day out.

What's possible when we admit that the mind occupies space that is rarely co-incident with the physical furniture, bright lighting, heating, air-conditioning, and even fun and pleasant surroundings? All of these merely create a level of acceptable existence. What about a space for the mind?

It can be described, and it can be enhanced by effective leaders who know that it all begins when key personalities share a vision and recognize the unique contributions of each individual. What's possible today when the incredible array of accessories for the mind in ever advancing technologies are carefully selected and combined in powerful combinations to enhance the capacity to see better, to hear better, to remember, relate, translate, and connect?

What's possible when growth is seen as the process by which people become connected with each other to operate at higher levels of organization and complexity? Or when simple indications like the angle of people's chins are seen as meaningful measures of emotion—or lack of it. What's possible when leaders take personal responsibility for lifting peoples' chins—customers, employees, suppliers, and associates, and admit that emotion and mental energy are synonymous? Recognizing that every single day is precious, that minds can be engaged and empowered with a shared vision, that mind accessories are available far beyond their current application, and that growth is the process by which people become connected and human aspirations and organizational results can become one.

It's that important. And possible.

Read this book with intention. The intention of developing your inner leader. Allow your mind to open to what is possible within you. Personalize how these concepts work for you and your team.

Join us on the journey of moving from where you are to where you want to be. From what is to what can be.

Think about the change you want to see, for yourself, your team, and your business. Think about what the future looks like if you were to make this change.

Why did you decide to read this book?

On the next page and throughout the book, feel free to write your answers and ideas.

Where are you right now?

What's your current situation? Describe where you are in your career and life and with any team or company you're leading.

Where do you want to be?

What are your goals/dreams/hopes? What does that future version of you and your team look like? How do you feel about it? What becomes possible?

Who are YOU?

Before we call you to the action of filling the gap between what IS and what CAN BE, let's look at WHO you are and the version of yourself that is needed to achieve what is possible for you.

There is a saying that originated with Paulo Cuelho, "Maybe the journey isn't so much about becoming anything. Maybe it's about unbecoming everything that isn't really you so you can be who you were meant to be in the first place."

As a leader in today's changing world, how are you accessing all of your true self? Be open to the business strategies here and how letting them change you is what will lead to optimal leadership transformation.

CHAPTER 2

THE BUSINESS CASE

Section 1: Leading Business Transformation

What do our teams want and need?

Contrary to what many leaders think their teams want, such as higher pay and perks, our research and survey, combined with a recent Harvard Business Review study, show that the following is really what drives top employees' interest, loyalty, and engagement.

They want:

1. Flexibility - options that include remote work with the ability to make their own choices relating to their hours and location
2. Well-being - resources to support mental health and well-being
3. Diversity - to work for a company that embraces inclusion, boosting diverse ideas, creativity, and productivity
4. Upskilling - the opportunity to learn and grow using collaborative tools and technology to offer ongoing skill development
5. Great leadership - a trusting, open, engaging environment
6. Purpose - including clear communication of and alignment with company values and mission. They want to know they are contributing to something bigger and meaningful.

They Want more freedom to integrate what they do into who they are.

They Need the tools, resources, support, and leadership to do just that.

As a leader in today's world, one focused on serving your people in a bigger, better, and more current way, the tools of Mind SPACE and the Seven Levels of Communication will help.

Leadership in Every Level and Every Employee

Leaders have a unique opportunity to make a big difference for their people and their companies. When we remove assumptions and ask different questions, we teach by example the qualities that will enhance leadership within each team member.

We have been drifting for a while and this gives us a chance to reset and rethink. Now we are asking:

"What qualifications makes travel necessary?"

"How do I interact with people best?"

"What does a meeting mean?"

"What does leadership mean to me?"

"How can we best serve based on what our people and clients most need?"

Hiring & Training

It's time to review how we hire, train, and even what we look for in candidates. New positions may emerge—for instance, a chief remote officer would be focused on engagement, consistency of culture, communication, and the resources required for virtual employees.

New ways of onboarding need to not only communicate policies and practices but also foster important team relationships. Creative cross functional team collaboration will be necessary. Companies may be tempted to include software that monitors workers, but we recommend taking the time to cultivate a culture of trust. Employees want increased flexibility and autonomy in how they work. That calls for releasing micro-managing in favor of clear expectations, ongoing communication, and confidence that you've made the right hiring decision.

We're moving away from top-down management, and instead listening to bottom-up ideation, and prioritizing inside out leadership. This means we encourage leadership in every level and from every employee.

Matt Bartelme, CEO and founder at Bart's Tree Service, is working on innovative ways to fill the talent pool. "We've been working with our local senators to fill the needs to train potential employees. There's a huge area of talent that we need to bring up." He also takes it upon himself to educate and mentor students about these jobs they may not even realize exist. "We go out to speak at elementary schools... It's amazing to see the reactions when we say we get paid to climb trees—amazing how many questions one seventh grader can hit you with."

In addition to planting these seeds years in advance, there are ways to positively and proactively view hiring right now that will help.

Dawn Penfold is president of Meetingjobs, a Cadre Company. She observes, "Hiring will take on new dynamics with a need to be fluid as we transition to an environment with remote, in-person, and hybrid jobs and meetings. The talent pool will be worldwide, offering the hiring official a more diversified choice of candidate and the opportunities will be more available to those that were not considered due to their location. Hiring officials should look at the person offering diverse skillsets instead of those that meet just the requirements of the available position. Those organizations that bring flexibility in where and how people work as well as hiring those with diverse talent will succeed in times of constant change."

These additional options give you a wider range of cultures to choose from...or to run from. One human resources director I know was appalled at a recent interview. She shared, "I'm looking for a next level position managing a team and found this role that checked all my boxes. It wasn't too far from the house, and we've learned that we don't need to go into the office every day anyway with this type of position. With some back and forth, I got the offer I was happy with and went into some final interviews." She starts to speak faster as she remembers, "As I'm interviewing with my soon-to-be boss through zoom, I noticed an air mattress behind her. She saw me looking and explained that when things get busy or there are storms or anything, they stay over. That's when I realized that commitment for her meant living in the office. I can't do that, and I wouldn't expect anyone on my team to do that!"

Shorten the Range for Goal Setting

Gone are the five- and ten-year plans set in stone. With such rapid world change we must shorten our range for goal setting. You can and should have a vision of the future but breaking it down into shorter more adaptable plans with built in tracking to assess and tweak as necessary is imperative. This is the new leader's toolbox. The ability to use goals as building blocks for the future.

Bonnie Marcus weighs in on this strategy. "Any long-range plans will require a plan A and B for each year."

In a changing world, time is compressed, we can't wait for problems to work themselves out. Information can be retrieved within seconds of the request, therefore solutions can be found and implemented more quickly. It becomes even more important to make sure we are asking the right questions in order to solve for the right problem.

Faster modes of working are cropping up, such as online business models, freelance work, remote communication tools, and ways to capitalize on making the global market more accessible. When we know ourselves, our people, and our business, we can choose the right tools that help us grow.

With all these choices, new and better ways of leading are imperative. That's why this book is relevant right now and in the future. It gives you the concepts, the tools, and the motivation to lead your team, your business, your life.

We must expand our minds to be able to have the capacity to not only keep up with but stay ahead of the integrity of our choices and the vision of what is possible.

Katina Athanasiou, former chief sales officer for a large cruise line, offers, "Throughout my entire career I made sure that I was confident in what I knew, what I said and that I had the data to back it up." She elaborates, "Everything was in a box with pretty wrapping. This year I had to throw that all out the window and say I don't know. I'm not certain how but we're going to get through it. I've had to rely a lot more on my gut and my intuition to help me and my team more than ever before."

Certain things matter now that were never even considered before. Empathy and authenticity are being embraced as the strengths they are, and different ethical concerns are opening dialogues that never needed to take place in the past.

For instance, there is a dichotomy between the ease and power of artificial intelligence to learn the needs of clients and the demand for a higher level of protection and security. Artificial intelligence is only one example of transformative technology that lives in the land of gray.

Authenticity has become a valued leadership trait. Transparency to be honest about what we can and can't do allows us to admit that we don't know all the answers. The result is that authentic leaders generate more trust and loyalty in their employees. Empathy has become another crucial tool to break down barriers that have limited connection.

Consider that these modifications in a leader's perspective and actions are not to be shied away from but instead to be embraced as the beneficial evolution it is. When we shift and own our thinking, we become empowered, therefore enabling us to empower others and serving an essential need in business today.

The solution lies within us. Awareness of what is and leading change to create what can be. Change isn't going away and the resiliency to navigate it is the most important and usable skill you can learn. A cultivation of that gut instinct Katina mentions is one element, along with heightened awareness, quick thinking, exceptional communication, and elevated questioning strategies.

As we lead our change strategies, we must remember that element of service. As leaders, we must know the impact our actions and our companies have on our clients, community, and the world. And that will keep us focused on the right path and help ensure a sustainable future.

To lead a team, a company, an initiative, or even yourself in your own life comes down to the ability you have to dig deep, to understand your current tolerance for discomfort as well as your capacity to expand.

Section 2: Foundation, Philosophy & Tools

The work from anywhere philosophy

This 'work from anywhere' philosophy includes non-location-specific workspace that opens opportunities, increases potential for profitability, and enhances quality of life. Benefits include removing time wasting and stressful commutes as well as flexibility in choosing where you live based on something other than proximity to an office. You can decide based on nearness to family, ideal weather, school districts, culture, cost of living, and a host of other important factors.

A good percentage of people don't want to go back to the office full time. "You can't put a price on the flexibility of remote work," says Human Resources Specialist Jesse Farmer. Other comments from clients include:

- "Why would I want to waste three hours of my day in a commute that ends with me having to pay for parking if I don't have to?"
- "I love being able to do my laundry while I'm working. I can't do that from the office!"
- "Being able to take a lunch break with my kids and my spouse is something I've never been able to do when working at the office. I don't want to go back."

To be fair we must also mention the additional pressure, more difficulty in building strong business relationships, and work/life balance challenges that can result from remote work. There will be a blurring of lines in not knowing where work and life begin and end.

It might be a difficult decision. However, it becomes infinitely easier if you have the tools and the leadership to maximize the opportunity and reduce the challenges. That's where Mind SPACE comes in.

Mind SPACE gives you a simple way to assess where you are so you know where to focus your attention and what improvements best get you to where you want to go more effectively, efficiently, and holistically.

Here's an example of a massive shift from physical to Mind SPACE—Silicon Valley. Proximity to others in the same industry for idea exchange, talent pool, and resource sharing is what facilitated the growth of Silicon Valley in the Bay Area in the 1970s and 1980s. And now, because of the changes in the world, we see various technology companies leaving that area to save money on real estate, taxes, and enhanced health and comfort.

Office space isn't going away completely. Productivity and creativity would falter without it. And the partnerships of corporations and cities are an integral part of our economy. The movement isn't mass exodus from physical space. The movement to Mind SPACE is in the increased element of CHOICE.

Choice is the balm to change. Mind SPACE is the solution to leading through it more successfully.

The growth of leaders, and expansion of their minds and tools, enables them to assess and make change according to their specific needs and the needs of the organization.

We spoke with Shing Wong, founder of the interactive event platform Ampslide. He said, "It depends on the company, product, and service they are offering as well as the culture. ...it will vary from company to company. I've seen some companies who work remote in general but then bring a team together for a one-month stint to deepen the collaborative bond because that's the best way for them to innovate."

He goes on to share, "There are pros and cons to virtual. A major benefit is that you can find talent from around the world. ... The con is that managers have to develop new skills and methods to integrate virtual and in-person teams into a cohesive culture, things that were not required when everyone was in-person."

Shing understands clearly that flexibility is one of today's most important leadership strategies. To stand out you must be adaptable to the marketplace and at the same time know clearly and be able to highlight what makes you different and valuable. These are part of the movement to Mind SPACE

We need a new way of looking at things that maximizes quality space for the mind. A way to capitalize on the best working environment while ensuring a balanced personal life. In particular—a way to assess and build a peak performance atmosphere.

We've developed a definition for Mind SPACE that facilitates high performance. It's a clear and simple way to assess where you are and where you want to go. It's effective for a solopreneur who is looking to build something bigger, an employee or manager looking to enhance their connection with others on their team or within their organization, or any level leadership in any size company.

The reason it is so versatile is that Mind SPACE can become an aspect of self-leadership.

Self-Leadership

Self-leadership is the way individuals lead their lives, from the goals set to the actions taken, and how they show up throughout it all. It comprises the core of who they are, including values, experiences, feelings, talents, and perspectives, as well as the way they conduct themselves consistently across all areas of their career, relationships, and life. There's a holistic nature to self-leadership. The growth that can come from awareness and adaptation is both all-encompassing and empowering.

Just one example of self-leadership is the discipline many have acquired while forced to work from home. As tempting as it might be, most people aren't sitting on the couch eating potato chips and watching TV during the day. They are working. For some, learning they have more discipline than they even realized has provided the conviction they needed to know this change can be sustained as a desired workspace over a forced one.

Another equally important tool for self-leadership is to know how to turn off the work and prioritize relaxation and personal relationships. It's a balance.

Self-leadership as we use it in this book includes a path of understanding yourself better and taking back control of your thoughts, feelings, and actions.

We mentioned that many people give up their power by allowing external situations to infect their mental state. They allow outside issues, beliefs, situations, and opinions of others to cause them to feel bad or take actions that aren't in alignment with who they are or who they want to be. Such as:

- When the economy, the weather, or someone else's opinion 'makes' us feel a certain way
- Or when others, with the best of intentions, tell us to remain safe and not attempt to reach a bold goal
- Or when we are kept from a position or opportunity due to someone else's limiting beliefs

The best leaders are those who manage their own mindset, emotions, and behaviors.

Leaders accountable for managing their own mindset, emotions, and behaviors are more able to effectively navigate change, communicate better, and set an example of leadership that inspires others. As leaders, the ability we have to align our actions with Mind SPACE expands our responsibility and our potential beyond what we once thought were our limits.

The more you can manage yourself, the more you can see the potential for that beyond self. Service focused leaders realize that we are not solo beings traveling a solo experience. There is something each of us does that is special and meant to be part of the larger whole. We are each intricately woven into the outcome of it all.

Leaders engage their teams in ways that expand something within each person to help serve a greater good. Mind SPACE is an instrument for change.

Michael Burke, Director of Conference & Travel Services for a major property & casualty insurer connects self-leadership, company leadership, and service with "Our company has always strongly encouraged community service. When trying to think of different ways to engage our employees, we want them to become part of the solution. One of the things that's kept them motivated is working with the community relations team to come up with what they want to do for employee events or to contribute to their favorite charity through our Community Heroes campaign. Creative ways to give back." This engagement has increased the company's ability to provide more meaningful service while simultaneously enhancing the morale and passion of the employees.

Mind SPACE is a tool you can use as an entrepreneur with a team or in leading a company or community initiative. The flexibility of it can open your mind to options and solutions.

The Power of Mind SPACE for Teams

There are three ways we define the environment of an organization.

1. One is physical, defined in terms of facilities and geography,
2. Another is organizational, described by mission statements, organization charts, department charters, and job descriptions,
3. The third is communication and relates to the way in which people are supported and stimulated by their environment to produce results. We see it as the most important.

Here we focus on refining the communication environment. We wanted something you can control and track that would affect change.

It is clearly perceived when communications are cluttered and frustrating. "Just get out of my way and let me do the job" has little to do with either the physical environment or an organizational structure. Instead you'll want to cultivate a supportive and helpful environment in which the power of the individual and organization can be productively directed.

We knew it would be important to breakdown steps into understandable and teachable components. These five basic elements create the performance environment of Mind SPACE. They include Shared Vision, Personality, Access, Connections, and Emotion—spelling out SPACE. Each of the elements can be defined, evaluated, and measured, making the invisible environment clearly visible.

When we add the power of self-leadership to these five elements, we have a compelling tool to assess and use in various scenarios. We can utilize it to direct ourselves, build stronger connections in both physical and virtual workspace, and take more effective actions that lead to higher performance and results.

Why Now? We can give a list of reasons where and why our current and future-focused, ever-changing environment is guiding us, but let's begin by looking back.

There is a story about 53 people who independently survived a "near death experience." They were interviewed by a psychologist who asked each of them what they recalled from the experience. Everyone remembered being there as a mental presence but not physically. In the near-death experience there was total separation of the mind from the body.

How many times have you looked around a conference table or classroom and noticed that at least half of the people were having a near death experience? They obviously are not fully present, their attention has 'left the building.' Attendees of virtual meetings are even less discrete... if their cameras are even on. Learning to ENGAGE ourselves and our people in any situation is imperative.

We want to align the mind and the body—with our own energy, in team meetings, during events, across the board.

People often tell us that they are capable of doing much more in the average day than they are allowed to do. They remember times of peak performance—working on a task force or special assignment—when they were exhilarated and delighted with their own work and with their contribution to the larger task.

They also remember the times when the workplace was not exciting or demanding, even those times when their minds tended to drift away to more interesting places.

To avoid frequent emotionally drained experiences and lengthen the times of peak performance, a manager must recognize peoples' ability to help create an environment where they can perform as a team, working in concert. This is especially important as we increase remote work.

A systematic way to define, use, and enhance performance.

A systematic way to define, measure, and improve the quality of communication in the workplace is needed. By capitalizing on the power of Mind SPACE we can enhance team performance. What we can measure can be replicated.

It's now time for every leader to come from a place of trust. To develop their people, share the Mind SPACE tool, exceed results, and enhance morale. The performance environment of Mind SPACE is meant to produce peak performance. This work may not need to take place in an office. But when you hold your teams accountable and allow them to perform in their peak, everyone wins.

The Mind SPACE concept and tool can help improve communication and results whether you are working in a physical location with other team members or remotely connecting through technology and devices.

Foundation

We both have been lifelong students of effective communication. With the research, philosophy, and behavioral and management strategies we've spent a cumulative 100 years cultivating, it would be tempting to make this book lengthy and complex. But our goal was to give YOU, our reader, actionable concepts and tools you can use right away to help you lead more effectively. You'll find Mind SPACE and the Seven Levels of Communication laid out simply in the following chapters to foster that objective.

We thought you might first like to see why it was important to us to communicate the message this way. It stems from this bonus strategy we'll simply call ABC.

Section 3: Effective Communication – As Easy as ABC

In traditional ways of doing business, improving communication has been one of the most important elements in achieving more sales, higher customer satisfaction ratings, and increased morale. It's also one of the primary dysfunctions in many struggling organizations.

According to a 2021 survey by Expert Market, 97% of workers believe that communication impacts their tasks every day. Communication can improve or reduce efficiency, morale, negotiations, production, and nearly every aspect of business, depending on how well you do it.

In our new era of change, modern leadership, and Mind SPACE, communication becomes an essential focal point. As distance between employees, vendors, and clients expands, effective communication becomes even more necessary. As leaders, we need to be aware of any discrepancies (nonverbal or verbal) between departments and levels.

There are difficult moments in business, such as a major world change like the recent pandemic or a reorganization that requires massive layoffs or even a shifting to a new foundational organizational system. These are the moments when leaders find communicating time-consuming and uncomfortable. It's often forgotten, ignored, or there's a feeling that someone else will do it or perhaps that employees already know.

In times of change, it is better to overcommunicate, even if it is "we don't know yet." It's not the words so much as it is the assurance. It's not what you say but how you say it.

It's effortless to tell people things are going great! Conversely, letting them know they're in for a bumpy ride is NOT easy.

Culprits behind lack of communication:

- Lack of information
- Uncertainty how the message will be received
- Lack of clarity in what comes next
- Other priorities
- Lack of time

This uncertainty is why leaders pull back. It's also why they must lean in. Take responsibility for the good, the bad, AND the uncertainty. Lead the way. Pave the path. And keep the team involved all the way along the journey. This form of leadership produces loyalty.

In working with teams that have or are going through change, one of the biggest requests employees have is the need for more and better communication. When teams thrive during these changes, there's often a direct correlation to the fact their leaders are open, transparent, engage input from the team, and offer a vision of a better future. A leader becomes a change manager through communication.

Besides during those major business changes, other areas of communication that can be challenging and need to be addressed:

- Developing consistent communication with prospects and clients across formats and styles
  - Marketing
  - Social media

- ○ Emails
- ○ Texts
- ○ Video chat
- Communicating your purpose and values
- Explaining benefits of services vs features
- Navigating the expanded ways we communicate using technology
- Engaging with staff and customers remotely missing the face-to-face feedback

Let's look at a communication story and bonus tool that led to a concept anyone can use. It will simplify your ability to relate and allow you to better communicate in all different scenarios.

As Easy as ABC- From Will's Perspective

From 1973-76 I was head of GE advertising nationwide, headquartered in Schenectady, NY. I didn't come from the advertising world, and as always, understanding what's working and why was very important to me. I pulled aside the best generalist, the best writer (see his personal story on page 36), and the best artist on the team.

I asked them to answer this important question, "Tell me how to rate an advertisement on a scale of 1 to 10?" They had two months to come up with the answer.

They went away and worked on it but had a very difficult time coming up with an answer. About a month later, they came back and said we have advertisements hanging all around the room and we can't answer your question. These gentlemen had years of experience and I knew they had the answer inside of them. After reminding them they had another month to go, I sent them back to the drawing board.

With one week to go, they came back again, having changed the question to "What makes communication in our advertisements effective?" Being clever, they broke it down to the ABCs of Communication. They said, "Communication is as simple as ABC. You must start with C… where C is your end user or your receiver."

- C is your customer or the person who is on the receiving end (conceive the proposition)
- A is your product or message and how the user needs it (strategize the proposition)
- B is the delivery system between A and C (dramatize the proposition)

Most people begin with themselves or their product or service. Success lies in **beginning with your receiver.** Finding out what the buyer/client/spouse (remember we're talking about any communication!) wants or needs. Many people start with their product or service's features. What *they* believe is great about it. But if they don't start with the receiver, they often miss the mark.

Next you go back to the beginning and **strategize the proposition**. How does what you do tie into and solve the needs of that receiver?

And finally, you **dramatize the proposition**, adding flair to the benefits, driving home the points. Thinking this through, you can see how this method can help with any type of communication.

As an example, let's look at one of the most effective ads of its time... for Wonder Bread.

Example

WONDER BREAD

RECEIVER
Q Who would be purchasing bread within the family?
A The moms
Q What would be most important to them?
A The health of their children.

STRATEGY
Q If focusing on healthy kids, would the taste, or the freshness, or perhaps a fun toy be MOST important?
A No, It would be that it's GOOD for them.
Q What else would busy moms like?
A Ease

DRAMATIZE
Q "Builds strong bodies 12 ways!" And did you know that Wonder Bread came up with the idea to slice bread to better serve these moms?
A It wasn't just their ad team but also their production team who understood differentiation! They looked at innovative ways to make mom's lives easier. Bread used to only come in loaf form. Wonder decided to slice theirs to make it faster and easier for moms to make sandwiches.

This slicing idea was so revolutionary that we talk about it today (*It's the best thing since sliced bread!*) and probably don't even know why... can you imagine not having sliced bread?!

Now let's move the example from ads to communication in general. Let's take decisions we made for this book as an example.

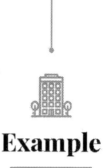

Example

WHERE'S THE OFFICE?

RECEIVER	
Q	For this book, we spent time thinking about the reader. What type of a leader might you be? What is your style? The things you need, what you like to do, what bugs you, and what goals you have.
A	We realized you would already be good leaders, ones who are motivated to improve, and who are willing to take actions to achieve your goals.
STRATEGY	
Q	Our readers want to move from good (or even great) leaders to extraordinary. But they don't have a lot of time to waste.
A	It was important for us to write a concise book that gets to the point and provides actionable takeaways.
DRAMATIZE	
Q	We know that stories make things interesting...
A	So we made sure to add stories to build connection.
Q	We know that people learn better and faster when engaged...
A	So we added ways and places for you to personalize the journey.
Q	And we know that reinforcement is often needed for real transformation to take place...
A	So we included online resources and follow up for you.

This time it's your turn:

Your Example

RECEIVER
Q Who is your target market? What do they most want? (This applies as well if your 'market' is another internal team or an individual.)
A
Q What other questions should you be asking?
A

STRATEGY
Q Continue thinking through how your product or service can help your client solve their specific pain or reach their unique goal.
A

DRAMATIZE
Q How can you drive home the point for your clients by communicating how what you do is unique and better?
A

The Story Behind the Story

You don't often get the chance to go back and ask an employee about what they were thinking or the process they used in the creation of a tool that has been used to success for years. But we had that chance. Our good friend Robert Lauterborn was one of the three who came up with the ABC concept. Here he tells his side of the story of Will's question and how the ABC concept came to be:

Frustrated by his perception that there was apparently no way to evaluate advertising beyond subjective judgements, Will Lewis assigned veteran art director Walt Brzoza and young hotshot copywriter—me (Robert Lauterborn), supervised by our superb creative department manager Bob Pulver, to come up with such a tool that could be taught and implemented to produce a consistently high creative output across A&SPO's nine U.S. offices and our six operations in Europe and Asia.

We were relieved of our line and client assignments and freed to concentrate totally on this one all-important mission.

Well, um, okay… what do we do now?

I set about reading everything that had ever been written on the subject of creativity and advertising evaluation—trade paper articles, speeches by recognized creative leaders, books and pamphlets, and everything I could dig out of the archives of associations such as the ANA, the Four A's, the Advertising Research Bureau, and the magazine and newspaper publishing entities. (Being primarily a business-to-business agency, we produced mainly print advertising rather than TV or radio, although we did want our method, formula, process, whatever it might turn out to be, to be applicable across all media.) I also interviewed the creative directors of several of the more famous advertising agencies.

What did I collect? Lots of opinions and a few subjective formulas, but no science beyond focus group research, which itself was hopelessly flawed. (Direct mail was the exception. They could test relative target audience responses to different approaches with A&B list mailings. That was the closest anyone had ever come to a predictive system, but that was obviously not applicable to other media.)

Meanwhile, Walt was collecting every print advertisement done by any part of the General Electric Company in the previous year, not just from our A&SPO group but also by BBDO (the company's corporate agency of record), Y&R (another Madison Avenue agency that had a couple of GE consumer product brands), and any outliers a rogue product department might have hired.

He also found out as best he could who the writers and art directors were for each ad. He mounted the ads on the floor-to-ceiling cork walls in his large office so we could study them. This was to be our lab. The ideas, approaches, insights, whatever we found that we thought might have some promise, we'd try to apply to these ads to see if it would help us not only evaluate but improve on the work.

I'm almost ashamed to admit that at first, we were thinking in terms of developing a set of rules, or rather two sets: Thou Shalt Do These Things To Make Great Ads and Thou Shalt Not Do These Things.

Silly us. Rules don't work. How many times have you seen a list headed "How to do great advertising?" If rules worked, there'd only be one list and we'd all have a copy. But how we really proved that rules don't work was in our wall-of-ads-lab.

Early on, we more or less ranked the work we'd collected. In the process we identified one particularly outstanding ad in the collection and said to each other, "There. That's the kind of work our writers and art directors ought to be turning out every time. Who did this beauty?" (Remember I said that Walt had tried to find out who the copywriters and art directors were for every ad on the wall.) So, we turned this one over and there were their names, Tony and Al, two of our most talented guys. Well no wonder.

So we skipped to the other end of the spectrum and picked out an ad so bad that we were embarrassed it ever came out of our shop. At the lowest common denominator for an ad you ought to be able to tell at a glance who is selling what to whom and why that person should buy. This one didn't even clear that low hurdle. "Okay, let's see who was responsible for this turkey," we said, and turned it over. You guessed it. Tony and Al. Uh-oh. So much for the value of rules.

Tony and Al don't need a set of rules to tell them how to do great advertising. They know how to do great advertising. Something in the process not only prevented them from doing great advertising, but it also caused them to do terrible advertising. We needed to figure out what that was. Back to the drawing board.

Walt and I worked wonderfully well together. We could take a so-so ad and between us could always raise it a level or two. I'd rewrite the copy and he'd redesign the layout and voila! Instant improvement. But some of the work we were looking at defied our best efforts.

Frustrated, we looked at the worst of the work on the wall and knew that there was no way even we on our best day could fix it.

"What's WRONG with this," we said to ourselves, and then one of us—we could never remember which one—said, "It's just out of focus."

And just like that we redefined our mission: How do we help our friends and colleagues to make sure that everything they do is IN focus? And FOCUS became our focus.

These gentlemen hit on something extremely important in their lab. Stimulated by a question to better understand a process in the hopes of incorporating the answer into a shared vision that could motivate a higher, more consistent level of performance.

In your desire to lead and/or communicate at an advanced level, begin with laser focus, and allow this focus to open you to new information that can be carried forth as part of your shared vision for the future.

In moving forward to our two primary tools—Mind SPACE and the Seven Levels of Communication, focus your attention on finding the ideas that will work best for you, your purpose, your vision, your team, your company, your world.

CHAPTER 3

MIND SPACE – DEEPER DIVE

In today's world, one of the biggest business transitions has been moving from our physical space. There was a necessary mass exodus from central offices that occurred at the time of the writing of this book. The COVID-19 pandemic forced people to reevaluate the way they ran their businesses and their lives. Changes needed to take place based upon the challenges this presented, as well as the options that were opening because of them.

Temporarily, and seemingly overnight, traditional workspace changed dramatically. People were conducting business from home, doing a wide variety of work roles and tasks right next to their spouses doing the same, all while home schooling. Overwhelm ensued. A new concept and way of navigating this transition was required. People were examining optimal ways to work both physically and mentally.

Whether you're reading this hot off the press as it's occurring or years later, the concept of cultivating Mind SPACE calls for better solutions to effective leadership and communication.

This idea of a movement out of our offices into a portable office or a conceptual space isn't as new as we imagine. We've been unwittingly planning for it for some time. With our technology getting smaller and smaller, we can fit all we might need to work right in our pocket. We have become invested in a remote workspace, carrying our work with us, on our person. This transition enabled an easier jump to it being WITH us to… It is WITHIN each of us.

"We are moving from physical space, connected by the motor car to conceptual space, connected by electronics." – from Will Lewis in Megatrends by John Naisbitt, 1982.

As typical, Will was ahead of the times in his thinking, and his friend saw the value in his wisdom. The seed was planted and all that has happened between then and now have been the sun, the water, the care that enabled the idea to blossom exactly in the time and space when it was required.

Section 1: Mind SPACE – Five Basic Questions and Instructions

We believe in the power of questions.

The best way to use this tool is to begin with the questions. We provide you ones that primarily relate to you as a leader in a company. You can start with those, or you can customize ones that align more with your personal experience and desired outcomes.

More instructions will come at the start of each exercise.

The FIVE QUESTIONS include:

1. What do we know about the clarity and acceptance of our Shared vision and values?
2. Is there a match between the Personality of each individual and the role the person is paid to perform?
3. Have we considered the Accessibility of whatever is needed for effective work, including the quality of accessories for the mind?
4. What is the quality of the Connections with other people?
5. How is the power of Emotion in our working environment?

You'll find additional questions along with these five as you work through Mind SPACE. An easy way to remember the five elements is with the acronym S P A C E –

Shared vision
Personality
Access/Accessories
Connections
Emotion

Performance Profile
Mind SPACE

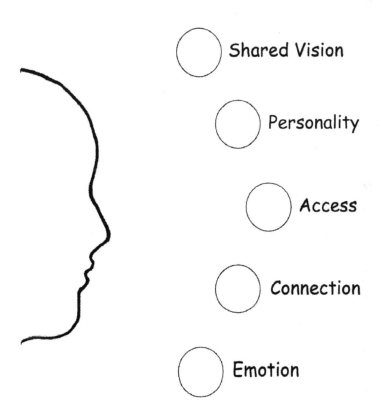

Shared Vision

Personality

Access

Connection

Emotion

Mind SPACE Instructions

Read each section to better understand the concept.

Choose an overarching FOCUS AREA: this is your primary focus and should be used throughout this particular Mind SPACE session. You can do this as many times as you like. Visit our resource page to download additional copies of the Mind SPACE tool. https://bit.ly/wherestheoffice

Focus area can be on:

1. Your growth as a leader
2. Your team dynamic
3. A specific challenge or goal
4. Other _____

Keep this focus area in mind throughout as you answer the questions, then RATE where you are according to the focus area you chose. Use this guideline (we recommend placing a sticker in the circle on the Mind SPACE Performance Profile).

Green - is a go and all is working well.

Yellow - means this is an area you may want to look into.

Red - means warning—there is a significant issue here that needs to be solved.

Take the sections one at a time. Read them to understand how it applies for you specifically.

Use the tool to assess your current situation. In order to help you move from where you are to where you want to go, we must begin with your existing state of mind and business.

The work area is for you to write out your thoughts in free flow idea storming fashion, which will lead to possibilities for a plan of improvement and priority areas to focus upon.

Section 2: Shared Vision

Shared vision
Personality
Access/Accessories
Connection
Emotion

> *"A vision is not just a picture of what could be;*
> *it is an appeal to our better selves,*
> *a call to become something more."*
> ~Rosabeth Moss Kanter

Shared vision and values—the biblical verse "without a vision the people perish" is timeless and reminds us that this is the basic element of the performance environment.

American psychologist John Gardner has said that one of the characteristics that sets "leader" managers apart from run-of-the-mill managers is their heavy emphasis on vision, values, and motivation. The articulation of vision and values can be done in many ways. The importance of the shared vision cannot be over emphasized.

You must have the vision of what is possible so that you can not only serve employees as they work in their physical or virtual space, but also serve the employees as they carry out their responsibilities as representatives of your company. A key element in our work with clients is to make the truth about the communication environment visible—a shared vision.

Todd Cherches, CEO of BigBlueGumball and author of *VisuaLeadership: Leveraging the Power of Visual Thinking in Leadership and in Life* shares that, "People are not motivated by facts and figures; they are motivated by a picture of a future that is different from – and better than – the current reality. Too many leaders try to inspire their teams to higher levels of performance by talking about hitting sales targets and rising quarterly earnings. But most employees don't really care about these things; they care about making a difference."

Todd continues, "Dan Pink, in his book, *Drive*, states that people are motivated by Autonomy (the freedom to do things their own way), Mastery (continuous learning and growth), and Purpose (doing work that matters). With that being the case, leaders need to not just "tell," but visually "show" their people how and why their collective actions will contribute to a better and a brighter future. And to do so, leaders can be more effective at getting their people to "see" what they're saying by leveraging the power of visual imagery and visual language. For, just as a picture is worth a thousand words, equipping, enabling, empowering, and inspiring employees to turn the shared vision into reality can, ultimately, be worth millions of dollars."

In the past, a common way for management to share a vision was to publish a "vision statement" along with a list of values. There are times when a visual is far more effective.

During the breakup of a large client, the corporate officer who had to take apart a headquarters organization was working under unusually intense pressure.

We knew that a written strategic plan was not the best medium for appealing to the emotions of the hundreds of people who had to work under these trying circumstances. Since the officer had a vision, we thought, "Why don't we use television to make the concerns, feelings, and the wishes of key clients come alive?"

We produced a brief video called *A Shared Vision*. Employees said that before they saw the video, they did not have a clear picture of what they were facing and what was expected of them. After seeing and hearing their perceptive and convincing leader and some important clients, they knew what they had to do and were eager to go with it. This was an effective way to distribute the Shared Vision of the company changes.

Since that time many years ago, there has been an explosion of television, video, and visual components overall.

From recent research by Hubspot: "Nearly eight out of ten marketers feel that video has a direct, positive impact on sales.

And 94% of marketers agree that videos have helped increase user understanding of their product or service, with 43% reporting that video has reduced the number of product support calls their company has received." It's exploded as a medium for leadership, vision, marketing, sales, and more.

Peg Thoms shares from her book *The Daily Art of Management*, "An organizational vision is a cognitive image of the future. It must be positive enough to followers to motivate them and elaborate enough that it provides direction for future planning." In deeper discussion with her, an important point emerges. True vision must come from a leader with the power to drive it down. They then must communicate it clearly to the people who have the capacity to execute it.

Envisioning a future of possibility isn't only for corporate folks. It applies in any area of business and life, providing clarity, hope, and something to strive for. Let's look at philanthropic work.

Whether you simply want to do good, are starting a nonprofit organization, or you are set to achieve any mission beyond you, shared vision is important. You may have created an idea on your own. It may be close to your heart and something you feel inspired to contribute to, but that doesn't mean it is yours alone. You'll want and need help to achieve it, and shared vision enables you to take the concept created in your mind and project it into the heart of another.

Visualizing the end result helps clarify and communicate it. It attaches emotion and commitment. Olympic athletes use visualization to great results. They see every move they plan to make during the competition ahead of time in their mind's eye. During the visualization they add other senses, such as the breeze blowing their hair, the scent of sweat, the roar of the crowd when they reach the finish line. This combination intensifies the visualization. This mental rehearsal prepares their minds by reducing anxiety and increasing confidence. Research has shown visualization activates the motor cortex, preparing the body as well.

Purpose driven leaders can use this tool to gain clarity and add emotion for deeper understanding when they communicate their vision.

One friend, the Regional Sales Director of a global company found that during the pandemic the mental state of employees was precarious, with morale low and fear high. He had a vision to reverse that.

He said, "As a whole, our company was working way more hours before. We were seeing visible burnout with team members."

He tells of the solution, "We started a weekly group meditation, an optional once a week meditation run by the director of operations. We also scheduled an additional couple of holidays where the whole company took an extra day off... A mental health day. It's gone over massively well.

"We've also instituted a biweekly happy hour that is optional. Every Thursday you can join a lunch group where you are randomly matched with others within the organization and results in a great, cross functional feel. Massive impact.

"The last piece was giving our people paid time off to get involved with local charities. There has been a substantial positive impact on the company. The positive state increased productivity. We've accelerated the natural progress of technology that would've happened in the next five years into one year."

We SEE the challenge, ENVISION solutions, SHARE the VISION, and take action for results.

Shared Vision is a pivotal point in all of our work. You'll see it in The Seven Levels of Communication as well. Keep your vision in mind as you work through all exercises.

Let's see where you are and how some of these examples might spark an idea for you. For now, simply assess where you are and answer the questions. We'll come back to fill in the gap with action later.

Ask yourself:

- As a leader, how am I fostering the vision for this team and company?
- Is the vision shared? Do we communicate it clearly, asking for feedback along the way?
- What do we know about the clarity and acceptance of our Shared Vision and values?

Fill out:

1) FOCUS AREA _____

2) RATE for Shared Vision are you:

   ❒ Green - is a go, and all is working well.

   ❒ Yellow - means this is an area you may want to look into.

   ❒ Red - means warning—there is a significant issue here that needs to be solved

3) Write

Next, spend time writing on the left side where you are currently with this element. What's working, what's not, and anything else you think is important as it relates to SHARED VISION.

Then spend at least as much time on the right side, writing where you could go. What possibilities exist? Who might be able to help you? What haven't you thought of yet?

Shared Vision

What IS	What CAN BE

Section 3: Personality

Shared vision
Personality
Access/Accessories
Connection
Emotion

> *"Personality is an unbroken series of successful gestures."* ~F. Scott Fitzgerald

Personality – the American Psychological Association defines personality as "individual differences in characteristic patterns of thinking, feeling, and behaving." Working to understand how the individual parts come together as a whole, the truly effective leader knows that you get better results if you match the job to the personality and not the other way around.

Akio Morita, co-founder of Sony Corporation, sometimes referred to American companies as being structured like brick walls while Japanese companies are more like stone walls.

"In an American company, the company's plans are all made up in advance, and the framework for each job is decided upon. Then the company sets out to find a person to fit each job. When an applicant is examined, if she is found to be oversized or undersized for the framework, she will usually be rejected. So the structure is like a wall built of bricks: the shape of each employee must fit in perfectly, or not at all.

"In Japan, independent recruits are hired, and then we have to learn how to make use of them. They are a highly educated but irregular lot. The manager takes a good long look at these rough stones and has to build a wall by combining them in the best possible way, just as a master mason builds a stone wall."

When you move beyond the role a person plays on a team or in an organization and into the fullness of their individual attributes, you can see the possibilities, the potential for each person to excel, but also how fostering that enhances the diversity in ideas, solutions, and collaborative excellence.

Fascinated by personality and behavioral patterns, we continue to research and better understand how the individual can combine with the appreciation of each members' differences to help teams move from disfunction to coexisting to thriving.

Many success stories and examples come to mind but one that stands out is a leadership team with a strong strategic planning initiative. This reorganization was one you'd imagine to be fairly seamless considering the proposed benefits to the majority of the employees and the organization as a whole. But it began as anything but. Meeting with the leaders of the team all quickly realized they weren't using their unique gifts to their best capacity. They were working against themselves and each other!

Using DiSC (a behavioral self-assessment tool originally based on the theory of psychologist William Moulton Marston) they found each member's strengths and natural style.

They enjoyed learning about themselves and each other. DiSC was used as a common language that enabled them to describe behaviors in an external, safer way to begin communicating effectively instead of the 'you vs me' mentality they had been cultivating. They realized they hadn't been using their strengths effectively. A positive note is that the tool helped them see how much diversity was already on the team. This may have been causing some initial conflict but as they learned more about their styles, they came to appreciate the diversity as a huge plus. They just weren't using it effectively. They exchanged a few roles and responsibilities, capitalizing on their individual strengths. That, combined with more open communication, helped tremendously.

The weaving of the individual personality characteristics into the fabric of a team makes a more beautiful design. The outcome is greater in whole than its parts.

A diverse and inclusive organization creates a more productive work environment that not only has better solutions and potential, but also enables development of opportunities for all employees without the fear of judgment and discrimination.

There are many tools you can use to understand and appreciate the personalities of the people you work with. The key is to come from a place of appreciation with a focus on how you can use this information to enhance each employee's career path and increase customer satisfaction, which both can lead to organizational productivity and profitability.

Ask yourself:

- As a member of this team - Do we embrace diverse experiences, cultures, ideas, and people?
- As a leader - Am I utilizing my strengths while partnering with others who complement and enhance what is possible beyond me?
- Is there a match between the <u>Personality</u> of each individual and the role the person is paid to perform?

"In this age of space time we seek multiplicity, rather than repeatability, of rhythms. This is the difference between marching soldiers and ballet."
~ Marshall McLuhan

Fill out:

1) FOCUS AREA _____

2) RATE for Personality, are you:

    ❐ Green - is a go, and all is working well.

    ❐ Yellow - means this is an area you may want to look into.

    ❐ Red - means warning—there is a significant issue here that needs to be solved

3) Write

Next, spend time writing on the left side where you are currently with this element. What's working, what's not, and anything else you think is important as it relates to PERSONALITY.

Then spend at least as much time on the right side, writing where you could go. What possibilities exist? Who might be able to help you? What haven't you thought of yet?

Personality

What IS	What CAN BE

Section 4: Access

Shared vision
Personality
Access/Accessories
Connection
Emotion

> *"Access to talented and creative people is to modern business what access to coal and iron ore was to steel-making."*
> ~Richard Florida

Access (or accessibility) deserves special emphasis. Today, the choice of accessories for the mind—electronic devices that can help a person see, hear, remember, relate, calculate, and connect—is practically unlimited. The problem at times is in integration. Or realization that it is possible. According to CEO of Hearing Access, Janice Lintz, the big issue is in the awareness that solutions exist, and they are simpler than one imagines.

It is important to remember that the mind, and not the equipment, software, tools, or other technology, is the terminal. Calling any device the terminal reflects a railroad mentality. The place with the tracks, such as Grand Central station, is called the terminal. But just as passengers continue on their journey through the station, so is the capacity of the mind extended through whatever device is provided for the user of the technology or system.

The designers of the technology must understand that it is only a piece of an increasingly complex task to provide ways to enhance the capacity of the mind. Remember the important question—What are you looking to access in using the automation or process?

- Increased productivity?
- More or better ways to connect?
- Innovative solutions?
- More time, information, communication capabilities?

Knowing what you're looking to access will help ensure you are making the right choices.

Have you ever seen someone jump into a new technology because it's the latest trend, only to realize that it had the reverse effect on the most important goal they were looking to achieve, gaining more time in their day for instance?

Have you ever seen someone avoid a new technology because it was uncomfortable and then be left behind in their role, business, or industry?

Have either of these two examples, been YOU?

If so, you're not alone. Whether you need to expand your access or your comfort zone, becoming aware of what tools you need to increase performance is the key.

During the pandemic people who were open to new tools, and were even ahead of the curve with access to programs as they were just coming out, were ahead of the game. If you were aware of, had access to, and even experience with apps like Zoom, Teams, Webex, and other virtual collaboration tools prior to COVID-19, you were more likely to ease through it. Being prepared doesn't just apply to the use of tech tools. Access to talent, getting education in the content most needed, and being able to obtain the resources and connections you need all played a part in the success of companies and their leaders.

Tracy Judge, CEO and founder at Soundings shared her experience related to access, "I have a network of freelancers. What I got interested in is how other industries were leveraging the freelance economy. Talent is going to look different moving forward. Tech companies and creators have been leveraging this for some time. What's unique about this is that project management tools and other structures in place enable us to look at what skills and experiences we need on our teams… And then we look at what of that experience has to be full-time and what doesn't. Can we build a business that we can plug-in talent on demand? This goes back to resilience and business continuity."

How does any of this apply to you? Can you think of other ways you can maximize access to help you thrive?

Ask yourself:

- What resources, tools, equipment, ideas, and skills do you need greater access to?
- Is there a clearer, better, faster path to closing the gap between where we are and where we want to go?
- Have we considered the <u>Accessibility</u> of whatever is needed for effective work, including the quality of accessories for the mind?

Let's find out.

Fill out:

1) FOCUS AREA _____

2) RATE for Access, are you:

❑ Green - is a go, and all is working well.

❑ Yellow - means this is an area you may want to look into.

❑ Red - means warning—there is a significant issue here that needs to be solved

3) Write

Next, spend time writing on the left side where you are currently with this element. What's working, what's not, and anything else you think is important as it relates to ACCESS.

Then spend at least as much time on the right side, writing where you could go. What possibilities exist? Who might be able to help you? What haven't you thought of yet?

Access

What IS	What CAN BE

Section 5: Connection

Shared vision
Personality
Access/Accessories
Connection
Emotion

> *"Communication—the human connection—is*
> *the key to personal and career success."*
> ~Paul J. Meyer

Connection- The old phrase, "it's not what you know but who you know," has truth in it. We could improve it by saying "It's who knows that you know what or who they need to know."

To the extent possible, people should communicate with anyone who can help get the job done. This innocent sounding idea violates the culture or even policy of some groups. Some companies are more prone to what we call a 'silo effect'—where teams or departments or levels keep best practices from each other and foster competitive gamesmanship.

As an organization expands, disconnections occur between layers, functions, and through geographic separation. As our world becomes more remote, these disconnections can reach epic proportions, creating serious problems.

Companies and individuals moving in that direction can't allow for the blocks that have traditionally been placed in the way of team bonding and relationship building. It's time to break down those barriers.

Our movement from physical to Mind SPACE has opened the eyes of many organizations. Mind SPACE will require MORE communication and better focus on creative opportunities to connect.

The importance of connection is made clear in George Land's book *Grow or Die*. Land says that "Growth is the process by which people become connected to each other in order to operate at higher levels of organization and complexity." Growth is seen not so much in physical size and financial terms, but in the capability and effectiveness of the organization.

To experience growth as defined by Land, an ongoing process for reconnecting people is needed. This process, if you don't have one, can be one of the first things you focus on in the table below. It's that important. Especially if your team is in part or whole working in a virtual capacity.

One of a leader's basic tasks is to engineer opportunities for connection over and over again as a part of a continual and evolving process. This facilitates the reliable bandwidth required for growth. Emphasis in this area can change a disconnected organization into a healthy and sustainable organism.

Discussing the balance of managing time, emotions, and connection during one of our focus groups, Sterena Strickland, Vice President of Sales for Access Destination Services, offered, "One of the culture changes for us is the connectivity of it. We have to figure out how to get everybody together with all the different schedules and continue the creativity." The scheduling Sterena mentions can be arduous, but it is worth the effort.

Isolation is a design for loneliness and narrow thinking. Connection is the conduit for expansive thinking that is mindful, beyond self, and of service.

When moving our 'office' from physical space to Mind SPACE, connection may seem like the first thing to go. It needs to consciously and continuously be cultivated. The skill of being a connector is one that can differentiate a leader.

Healthy connections in a company lead to more honesty and trust. Ideas and information are exchanged more freely, and this increased flow of productivity and positive energy can have a direct impact on the bottom line. When leaders come back to why we need to focus on opening the lines of communication and connection, it's easier to prioritize it.

Connections are equally as important for individual leaders. Being open and able to connect to the right people for mentorship, jobs, new business prospects, simple networking, and opportunities for learning and development is imperative to success. We aren't islands. We are humans, meant for connection.

The Phoenix community was started to support the massive influx of those in transition during the pandemic. It has had some outstanding success stories. They came for the confidence tools and expert interviews but found an even greater benefit of the community conversations to share best practices and find camaraderie and opportunities to build a network and partnerships.

How can you as a leader benefit from purposeful connections? We recommend building a *Connection List.* A list of people who are your top go-to people in various situations. Include a mentor role for advice, a new idea person for creative discussions, a reality check person, a company leader, and others. Start thinking about the connections that will help you most now.

The loneliness that occurs with prolonged disconnection can have the adverse effect of causing us to draw in upon ourselves, starting to doubt our ability or desire to connect. Isolation breeds isolation. We become too comfortable being alone.

Awareness of the barriers to true connection is essential. Whether those barriers are internal, as in growing self-doubt and fear that we can't reach out to others, or external, as in corporate blocks to keep a traditional organizational structure. In either case, the barriers must be removed.

Because connecting:

- Sparks ideas
- Releases stress
- Builds trust
- Opens minds
- Solves problems
- Leads to clients
- Grows revenue
- And even improves immune systems!

Ask yourself:

- Have we fostered an atmosphere of trust and the value of human connection?
- Do we have open lines of communication to connect to the people who can help us get our jobs done?
- Have I personally created a 'connection list' of people within and outside of the organization who can help me grow?
- Have I encouraged my team to do the same? And facilitated connections for them?
- What is the quality of the Connections with people we need to do our jobs and further the business goals?

Fill out:

1) FOCUS AREA _____

2) RATE for Connection, are you:

   ❒ Green - is a go, and all is working well.

   ❒ Yellow - means this is an area you may want to look into.

   ❒ Red - means warning—there is a significant issue here that needs to be solved

3) Write

Next, spend time writing on the left side where you are currently with this element. What's working, what's not, and anything else you think is important as it relates to CONNECTION.

Then spend at least as much time on the right side, writing where you could go. What possibilities exist? Who might be able to help you? What haven't you thought of yet?

Connection

What IS	What CAN BE

Section 6: Emotion

Shared vision
Personality
Access/Accessories
Connection
Emotion

> *"Our emotions need to be as educated as our intellect.*
> *It is important to know how to feel, how to respond,*
> *and how to let life in so that it can touch you."*
> ~Jim Rohn

Emotion - So often in management, emotion is thought of as something to be avoided. Have you heard the derisive expression, "don't get so emotional?" People are encouraged to leave their feelings at home. To be emotional is often seen as unprofessional, yet in truth, emotion is synonymous with mental energy.

Most people now realize that repressing emotion isn't the powerful stance we once thought. True power comes from being able to understand and harness our emotions to serve us better.

You can use emotion to

- become passionate about a worthy cause.
- build connections and deepen relationships.
- generate a calm, happy, or motivating environment.
- rally a team toward a common goal.
- create a buying space that excites clients.
- affect many other positive outcomes.

Look at the word emotion and within it you will find motion. Movement, energy, and emotion are tightly woven. When you are in a strong state like anger or fear, it can cause you to become immobilized. The best and fastest way through that feeling is to move your body. The movement generates energy which releases the fear and opens the mind to options.

You can use this knowledge to create a toolbox. Exercise, stretching, getting outside, or simply moving from one space to another can free you directly and immediately. Once you free the immediacy of the constriction that negative emotion can yield, then you can return to productive thought and action.

When working with and leading teams, the awareness of how to recognize and best use our emotions is the basis of emotional intelligence.

Changeologist and founder of The Trampoline Group, Alan Ibbotson relates, "I've been an Emotional Intelligence coach for over 10 years, and not only have I seen dramatic improvements in my clients - but I've also felt them in myself too. I have found that teaching and coaching others has been a wonderful way to hold myself accountable for the disciplines of EI as much as it has been about helping my clients.

"People are often surprised when I use the word discipline in relation to Emotional Intelligence, but I have learned just how much discipline is involved in labeling my emotions, controlling my impulses, and regulating my responses to the myriad of challenges that life continues to throw at me. The very foundation of EI is emotional self-awareness and to get good at that, I've had to develop a regular mindfulness practice. This has been a game changer in creating just enough time and space after a trigger to ensure I'm responding, not reacting from the low bar of my own nervous system."

Alan continues with a focus on results, "I've seen remarkable results in executives who have been willing to do the work - from the Executive Director who managed to turn around a huge company-wide morale crisis by building their self-confidence and finding their voice, to the CEO able to stop a mutiny on his executive team and harness the underlying issues as a growth opportunity for all, to the CMO who was able to successfully rebuild her relationships and reputation after getting hammered by her peers during a 360° review.

"Emotional Intelligence is the art of recognizing our emotions, how they're affecting us – and by extension people around us – so that we can be more conscious and deliberate about our responses. It takes courage, patience, humility, and persistence. But, by definition, it means that we are holding ourselves to our own highest, best standard, giving ourselves the gift of accountability for walking in our own values as leaders, colleagues and family members. Put simply - we are all at our best and most authentic selves when we are self-aware and emotionally intelligent."

"Conflict creates the fire of affects and emotions—and like every fire it has two aspects: that of burning and that of giving light. Emotion is the chief source of all becoming conscious there can be no transforming of darkness into light and apathy into movement without emotion."
~Carl Jung

Rebel transformative leader, Luisa Ferrario shares, "Teams and organizations are living organisms. As entrepreneurs and business leaders, we love them, we invest in them, and we give them so, so much to let them expand and thrive. So far so good… But what about the pain, the worrying, and the frustration when - as hard as you can try - your team and company's climate and results do not show up as expected? What about that gut feeling that whispers about a resistance beyond your understanding that is holding things back?

"Here is something I've learned from many experiences of helping entrepreneurs and business leaders transform their teams and organizations: Under the surface of most of their issues, you'll find that teams and organizations are just functioning from a percentage of what is truly possible, because of trapped emotions due to hidden forces they are unaware of, but that actually rule relationships and lead the business in their place. I call these hidden forces Board Of Transcendent, Transformative Officers and they can be either constructive or destructive. Unmask them and remove the last obstacle to take your team, business, and lifestyle to the next level."

To unmask these trapped emotions, you must first become aware that they exist. Then you need to go that extra step and ask yourself, "How am I contributing to the emotion on this team and in this business? What else could I feel to enhance team performance?"

There are two basic ways to motivate people—one is with heat and the other with light. Typically, the leader who applies the heat is autocratic and insecure, insisting that people do it his way, regardless of the value of the opinions of others.

The leader who enlightens by sharing a vision and inspiring people to do their best knows there are several ways to achieve the same goal. The leader who works with heat must always be around to apply the heat. The leader who helps others see the light knows that her enthusiasm is contagious and will spread without her constant presence. Both types of leaders affect emotion. Try asking:

- Does my company appreciate the connection between emotion and energy?
- Am I accountable for my own mindset, emotions, and behaviors?

The leader who constantly applies the heat generates quick bursts of negative reactions followed by smoldering ill will. Imagine the energy required to lead teams this way? Especially those that span remote, in-person, and hybrid environments.

The leader who enlightens creates a positive reaction that is strengthened with every achievement. This light focused leadership has the capacity to strengthen relationships and connect no matter the location.

Successful leaders know that people are most productive when morale is high. Emotion is the essence of creativity. Creative emotion is very easy to measure just by looking at the angle of people's chins. When emotions are high chins are up. The ability to create that space can be improved by understanding ourselves better (because we create the space) and becoming more mindful of the emotional reactions of others.

One of the most important elements of self-leadership is this ability to become aware of your emotions in time to consciously adapt. While this is the final letter in the Mind SPACE acronym, it certainly isn't least important.

It drives how we feel, therefore how we act. And as leaders this has a powerful impact on those we touch. Remember that the office is 'a service done for another' and we influence and inspire others whether we're alert to it or not. Become aware, and consciously choose the way you show up in the world.

That's leadership.

Ask yourself:

- How is the power of <u>Emotion</u> in our working environment?
- Is there anything I can do to become and foster more emotional awareness?

Fill out:

1) FOCUS AREA _____

2) RATE for Emotion, are you:

 ❏ Green - is a go, and all is working well.

 ❏ Yellow - means this is an area you may want to look into.

 ❏ Red - means warning—there is a significant issue here that needs to be solved

3) Write

Next, spend time writing on the left side where you are currently with this element. What's working, what's not, and anything else you think is important as it relates to EMOTION.

Then spend at least as much time on the right side, writing where you could go. What possibilities exist? Who might be able to help you? What haven't you thought of yet?

Wilford A. Lewis & Heather Hansen O'Neill

Emotion

What IS	What CAN BE

Section 7: The Story

The Process

The five areas covered include shared vision and values, personality, access, connections, and emotion which define an environment for the mind.

By answering the five questions in both words and color displayed on the unique form of the Performance Profile, a powerful picture of the gap between what is and what can be is created. (You can find the profile again at the end of the book or get an electronic copy with our resources link) The exercise can be revealing. And the colors will guide you to prioritize most important actions first.

In a seminar of Illinois educators, one of the counselors used red to answer the questions about personality and emotion. His response made it clear that he was not in the right job. He opened his brief discussion of the exercise by saying, "You have connected my head with my gut."

While some of the takeaways were related to individual leaders like this gentleman, the outcomes for company management were where most of the shifts took place.

It is an axiom of management that the people who are best qualified to solve the problem are those who work with the problem. This can be tricky. We have to reveal the problem in a constructive and positive way so that people know that they are seen as part of the solution instead of the problem. Asking people questions that must be answered with thoughtful, rational answers is not enough. What is needed is a way to display the feelings as well as the facts so that the resulting changes not only improve organizational results but also increase the vitality of the individuals involved. That's where the color comes in. Using color in the assessment of where you are attaches you to the emotion of the results, freeing the mind to respond without judgment.

The power of the Performance Profile comes from the combination of logic and creativity, left brain and right. The holistic nature of it engages everyone to move from what is to what can be.

Creation- a first-hand look at the exercise of creating the Mind SPACE concept from Will's perspective.

Years ago, there was a focus on improving physical space and I knew from my business experience that the real key to growth and success was in the enhancement of Mind SPACE. I began thinking about what was important in a successful organization.

The way and order in which I came up with the method wasn't linear. It was a process of the mind. We thought you might be interested in hearing the order and how it came to be.

First, I came up with *access*. It is important to be able to access the resources, technology, people, and equipment you need.

Then I thought about *connection*. The best companies allow for you to make connections within an organization. Including interdepartmentally, in various levels of management, with clients, and throughout the entire organization without feeling like you're going to be penalized.

Next there was the idea of a *shared vision*. When a shared vision, or a common why or purpose, is effectively communicated, everyone can work together at a higher level. And it has more meaning for all involved.

And then I thought of an element that was somewhat foreign to companies at the time. The emotional side. The *emotional quality* or culture of an organization can make or break them. Is it supportive, destructive, encouraging, harsh…? This top-down positive emotional quality of a company can be felt throughout, and is key for success.

I realized this acronym when put together in a different way spelled CASE. There are case studies of the best companies where you can see these components played out. I worked with and shared this concept to great success for several years.

But a while later, I felt as if there was something missing. Thinking it through, I realized that *people* are crucial. Meaning when we think about the individual, not just people in the sense of a role but the **personality** of the individual that makes them unique and different. That diversity must be taken into account!

Looking back at my process, I rearranged the letters again, and realized I had come full circle. The acronym was now SPACE. Completing the loop back to my original intention to help companies enhance their Mind SPACE."

How Mind SPACE worked in the world of the FBI

The FBI wanted to use the Mind SPACE concept in a workshop, attended by the Director of the Bureau and his nineteen senior executives.

Each person was handed three sheets, labelled:
Management 100 people
Agents 2,000 people
Support Staff 22,000 people

After hearing the definition of each element of Mind SPACE, the leaders were to respond with their assessment of each with one of three colored stickers, green (good), yellow (so-so) or red (not so good), for each area and group of people. After they filled in each of their responses, they held up their papers so that all could see.

Results of the Management and Agents' charts were predictable with varied responses. Results they gave the Support Staff was astounding. Every circle on this page, by every executive was RED.

Can you imagine the Director looking at the responses including his own? He said, "Either we have a problem and don't know it, or we have a problem and now we know it. In either case, WE HAVE A PROBLEM." And he humbly smiled.

The official comment days later came. "Thank you for the thought-provoking presentation at our recent Executive Conference Retreat. The stimulus that you provided crystalized our thoughts throughout the best retreat ever. We are now ready for long range planning."

As you can imagine, "best retreat ever" coming from the FBI, a world class organization was uplifting. The Director, Judge William Webster, later took charge of the CIA and brought Mind SPACE to that organization as well.

Once you evaluate where you are and understand the areas most in need of support and improvement, it won't be long before you recognize that better communication is needed to move forward into where you want to go.

> *"86% of corporate executives, educators, and employees*
> *cite ineffective communication and poor collaboration*
> *as reasons for failures in the workplace."*
> ~According to recent Expert Market survey

The Seven Levels of Communication is the natural next tool to assist your progression.

CHAPTER 4

THE SEVEN LEVELS OF COMMUNICATION

The Seven Levels of Communication

7.	Out of the blue	Imagination, insight and intuition, all illuminated by the skylight of the mind.
6.	Shared vision	A call to action that evolves from a keen understanding of what is and what can be.
5.	Understanding	Connections between people. The finely woven web of the corporate culture.
4.	Knowledge	"Know-How" -information combined with experience.
3.	Information	Data in context- form imposed upon unrelated facts and figures.
2.	Data	Random facts and figures, the fragmentary residue of processes and procedures.
1.	Turf	Defense of, or pride in, one's own territory.

As you navigate this leadership journey, there will be expected bumps and challenges. The radical changes required to lead teams of people from the traditional view of an office to the office being within requires you to not only demonstrate this new level of leadership, but also communicate new expectations and elevate your people to leaders themselves.

Enhanced and innovative communication strategies are called for to keep up with and stay ahead of the changes.

These Seven Levels show you a progression, the goal, and the potential of what can be at the top levels. They also take into account our humanness and the dance that naturally happens. Like the two-step, you may take a step or two forward, then one back in order to move forward again.

The key is to become aware of where you are and what is needed in different scenarios. Then you can use the tool over and over again to improve each interaction and create space for you and your team to grow.

Section 1: The Seven Levels of Communication – TURF

Turf - defense of or pride in one's own territory. At the bottom of this metaphoric ocean is the floor—all that is—what we call turf.

The definition of turf is an area regarded as someone's personal or business territory, home ground, or sphere of influence. Turf is the return to gut instinct. The protection of what's ours. Birds sing, dogs mark their territory, and people put up fences and walls.

This concept, while not something one would strive for, is important to recognize. Because it is based in impulse, emotion, and defense, much turf-related communication isn't rational. It's in our nature; it's our predisposition to battle for what we believe is (or want to be) ours. Territorial disputes in claiming land often leads to war, for seemingly illogical reasons.

In business, there is more time spent at this turf level than one might want to admit. You might be surprised by the sheer 'none of your business' mentality which fosters competition and blocks collaboration. Turf defense can be companywide. It can take place between individuals who are working together but differ in their perspectives, style, or perception of significance on the team. It could occur between departments who don't understand the needs of the other department, value what they bring to the table, or fear they will take credit.

Many shy away from sharing best practices based on this concern of someone else taking credit for their ideas or their work. We often see teams working on the same project in silos as if it's a "who can get to the answer first" philosophy instead of a process of "if we worked together, we'd all get to a better place more effectively and efficiently."

How do you know if you are leading a team that is communicating in Turf silos?

What does it look like? Your team members are communicating only with each other or vertically with those directly above or below them. There is little communicating between members of other teams, and if you have a desire to do so, blocks will be up.

How does it feel? It feels hard to get the information you want. You may feel alone, and you will feel less trust and confidence in your management.

What are the outcomes? You'll find less innovation in companies who work in silos. Productivity will be lower, and morale can be affected. The customer also often suffers because they don't get an experience that is consistent. Ultimately, this could impact the bottom line of the company.

Continue moving up the Seven Levels in your communication to increase collaboration and reduce these turf 'wars.'

A very different concept from silos and turf stems from South Africa—it's called Ubuntu. The presence of **ubuntu** is still widely referenced. It's a term from the Nguni languages of Zulu and Xhosa meaning, "a quality that includes the essential human virtues of compassion and humanity."

The Ubuntu story we know included the phrase, "I am, because you are" and was symbolized in a tale about a foreigner coming to visit the children of the tribe. He placed a huge basket of fruit at a point in the distance, encouraging them to run to it, with the first to reach it getting all the fruit—a great competition!

But the children held hands and walked toward the fruit, sitting together to enjoy it. The foreigner didn't understand. "Why didn't you try to win all the fruit?" And the children responded, "How could one of us be happy with the fruit if all of the others are sad and without?"

Just as that gentleman couldn't understand Ubuntu, those children would be quite confused by the U.S. focus on competition. While friendly rivalry can be an effective tool to enhance sales and innovation, staying in the land of 'turf' can be dangerous.

We've all encountered at one time or another someone who was obviously working from this mentality, "It's my turf, my responsibility, and I don't care about your feelings." Constructive exchange is impossible with people who will not budge from their turf.

On the other hand, there is a positive side of turf—a respect and pride of one's place in space. Every one of our levels of communication has a positive element. And for turf it is this aspect of responsibility. It's all in how it's used that can cause the issues.

Leader POV: You will find individuals for all the other Leader POV's but the best example for the Turf level of communication and the transformation that can come from acknowledging and changing it is an entire manufacturing company.

One corporate client entrenched in the Turf level of communication was a manufacturing company with locations in New York, Illinois, and South Carolina. These locations were not only working as their own entities without regard for the others, but they had negative connotations of the others' objectives and often blamed each other when a client called with an issue. They did a customer survey, and the scores were terrible! They knew they had to make a change, so they called us.

The walls needed to come down. Everyone had to come together and remove incorrect perceptions of the respective teams, returning to their common purpose. Opening the lines of communication and encouraging respectful, honest discussion between departments helped. For example, the sales department learned exactly what production needed and why, which encouraged them to set realistic expectations with the clients and lowered the number of irate calls customer service had to field.

The leaders had typically taken a 'hands off' approach, but when they heard how lost and unappreciated most team members felt they dove in, started moving meetings (quick meetings while walking either through the plant or outside on nice days), a full company run/walk to benefit cancer, and office hours focused on solutions and positive reinforcement. This helped to improve morale within the company as well as client perception and satisfaction overall.

This company was interacting strongly in Turf when we met. They moved up the levels of communication with emphasis on information, understanding, and even shared vision (which you'll see shortly). See if you can find your own examples as you learn about each of those levels. Notice times that an example may sound like the way you and your company are communicating. Making these connections will help you fully integrate the power of each level.

Turf communication can be found over and over again in organizations. No one wants to be the first to share their 'secrets,' their best practices. There's an undercurrent of 'selective' communication. There could be metaphorical backstabbing and a toxic energy. But when they see the detriment, this has on them individually as well as the company, they begin to lower their guard. With the intention to improve or serve a greater need, answers come, and exponential growth occurs. Leaders become more open and vulnerable, the people thrive, and the whole company excels.

Section 2: The Seven Levels of Communication – DATA

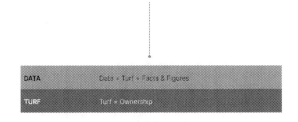

Data- This level has experienced the greatest transformation through the years since the creation of the levels. When computers were first used in business, the process was called DP or Data Processing.

By definition, data is "information output by a sensing device or organ that includes both useful and irrelevant or redundant information and must be processed to be meaningful." The power isn't in the data. It's in the insight you gain from it. This will be very important as we move forward.

Raw data, data files containing the fragmentary residue of processes and procedures of both the current and the old organization, is unfiltered.

Just as the archaeologist picks away at the layers of rock, so have the archaeologists of today come to understand our culture by decoding old computer discs. Data is, by definition, historic. We have no word for "future data." While data may be 'historic,' history as we see it today is a nanosecond ago.

The evolution of this data section has changed greatly over time and heavily influences the Seven Levels. Our desire is to give data the respect it deserves and also stay true to the fact that it remains appropriately placed and is in proportion to the other levels.

Data's growth and raw significance has expanded exponentially; however, the need for the levels that follow to balance it is even more important than ever before.

There are many positive components of data collection. Google Earth, for instance, enables students to visualize global learning and environmental applications. The ease in GPS navigation and house hunting are just the beginning of what is possible. The application utilizing the data is more important that the data on its own. The biggest collectors of data like Google, Apple, Facebook, Amazon, and Yahoo recognize and are seeing the profit of this big data collection business.

There is so much information to sift through with major ethical implications of what is being collected and how it's used. It can be frightening. Leaders need to use their power of discernment in Mind SPACE and take responsibility for how it's being implemented.

Remember to come back to service and connection.

- What is the purpose of the data?
- How are we using it?
- Are we considering rights and humanity?
- As leaders of the future, are there additional considerations you need to keep in mind?

A Leader's POV: Daniela Fazoli (Dani) comes from the hospitality sales world and made a conscious choice to dive deeper into data as a career, "There has been an explosion of data and data-driven decision making in companies across all fields and industries (much beyond scientific studies), and this is not a trend.

"Data driven decision making is here to stay and if you think Big Brother is out there watching you, let me also tell you he has a sister, a mom and a dad! There is nothing that we do nowadays that is not being recorded, analyzed, processed, picked apart and then sold for one purpose or another. Unless you want to go live in the mountains as a hermit, you are in the grid! If I am in it, I might as well benefit from it!"

Dani shares why she decided to go back to study data analysis, "For me, going into business analysis means bringing my business background to new technologies that allow me to process it, which is a huge advantage over just interpreting it. It is also about becoming more independent, and more needed in the marketplace. It seems to be a great middle ground between being in business and becoming a programmer.

"This new skill set will open many doors for me professionally and personally. In addition, going back to the "grid," evolution is happening at a fast and furious pace, and 80% of the professions of the future have not been created yet, so it is also about getting to the front and center of something that may take a completely different shape in the next 10 years. I surely do not want to miss this boat. I want to be part of the process, and I want to learn more."

She closes with, "This field is about the present, the future, hope, aspirations, realization, growth and so much more."

Daniela has decided to battle the beast of data by joining it. By learning more and being part of the push to move forward ethically and profitably.

Section 3: The Seven Levels of Communication - INFORMATION

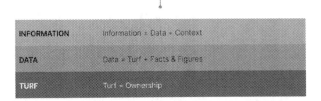

INFORMATION	Information = Data + Context
DATA	Data = Turf + Facts & Figures
TURF	Turf = Ownership

Information- The phase after Data Processing in the computer era was called Information Systems. Information is data in formation— data in context form, imposed upon unrelated facts and figures.

Bart Berkey, keynote speaker and author of *Most People Don't... And Why You Should* shares this story. "When geese travel, they almost exclusively fly in formation as a flock. They take turns leading based on the needs of the group. A goose or gander that is particularly good at navigation will lead when the group is lost, just as one that is exceptional at finding food will take the helm when the group is hungry. As a result of this formation (in a "V" shape), the entire flock can fly 70% farther and more efficiently than if each goose flew alone. Effective and efficient by working together!"

This story and this level of communication guides a leader to contemplate, "Do I have the right people in the right positions with the right information?"

One example of using data and turning it into information that is timely and of value to people comes from Michael Dominguez, CEO of Associated Luxury Hotels International (ALHI). During the pandemic, the meeting and hospitality industry was hit hard. There was chaos because of a lack of understanding about what was real, what was true, what was helpful, and what was significant. Michael had a long track record of being an expert in trends. He collected data and assimilated it into information in a way that was not only easy to understand but also valuable and inspiring. He had been doing this for years.

During the pandemic, Michael focused on the science and the facts when people were allowing emotion and dissent to cause stress. When he recommended the commonsense strategy of making decisions today based on solid goals of where you want to be tomorrow, people listened. When a trusted authority takes data from the top reliable sources and combines it with a passion for your specific industry coming from a perspective of service, the information provided eases your mind.

As the CEO of a company who depends on face-to-face events, Michael had every reason to be concerned and follow the mass appeal of fear. But he didn't. He turned the data into valuable information, and led his company and ultimately the industry to a place beyond fear...to action.

Data is the informal mind—information brings order and context to it. What helps to provide the context which creates information from data? *The question that you ask makes the response become information to you.*

For example, 55 is a number (data). How the number is applied gives the data meaning: an age, a speed limit, the weight of a child you need to lift, etc. Taking that a step further, setting the speed limit at 55 was information used to change a behavior. President Nixon was the one to mandate that speed limit in 1974 as a response to an oil embargo. The intention was to force Americans to drive at more fuel-efficient speeds. More information adds texture.

If you remember that questions enable you to move the data into information, you know that cultivation of the right questions is what will move you up the levels.

The appropriate question can move you from staying stuck in the problem (Why me?!) to options and solution (Who can help me solve this today?).

- What is the biggest challenge you are currently facing?

- What questions are begging to be asked?
- What is the goal you're looking to achieve?
- Are there questions that can help you prioritize or systematize the fastest or best track in getting there?

Make a list of starter questions here that can help you expand the possibilities for you and your business by opening your mind to new ideas, options, and solutions:

A Leader's POV: It's important to gain information and ideas from our people, but it's not always that simple.

Looking to solve this was Chief Idea Guy at The Growth Engine Co, Bryan Mattimore. He came up with the following idea in response to this question from one of his manufacturing clients. "I want the hourly workers on our production line to generate innovative ideas for cutting costs or even growing the business," said the president, "but I don't have the luxury of doing brainstorming sessions and taking them off the line for even a half hour. Got any suggestions?"

Bryan said, "This was definitely a challenge! We knew a typical suggestion box was unlikely to work. Suggestion box programs fail not because of a lack of initial employee interest or enthusiasm, they fail because the process for managing and following up on the submitted ideas isn't as rigorous as it needs to be."

Bryan knows that asking the right question can result in a great solution. So he asked, "Could we create a kind of "interactive" suggestion box where submitted ideas could be easily and efficiently built on by others?' It turned out we could. The ingeniously-simple solution is a personal, team, departmental, and/or organization-wide interactive idea suggestion and idea building tool we call the Whiteboard Technique."

Here's how the Whiteboard Technique works: The manager looking for new ideas posts a blank whiteboard in a public venue: outside his office, near the water cooler, next to the elevator, the cafeteria, wherever. Next, he decides on a creative challenge, and writes the challenge in the center of the whiteboard. The challenge could be anything from how to cut costs or invent new products, make work more fun, or create new marketing promotions.

Then the manager and his coworkers, over a pre-determined time—usually seven to ten days—write down ideas on the whiteboard. These "ideas" could also include creative thought starters, questions, drawings, wishes, areas to explore, and interesting factoids relevant to the creative challenge.

Each successive day, co-workers are encouraged to add new creative thoughts and ideas to the whiteboard.

We have discovered an advantage the Whiteboard Technique has over even traditional brainstorming sessions is creative "soak time." Time allows the wonderful pattern-finding, idea-combining ability of the human mind to work its magic.

After the allotted seven to ten days, the ideas on the whiteboard are summarized, and recommendations are then made to senior management as to which ideas should be pursued further. The output from the whiteboard can also be used as creative fodder for an in-person team ideation session.

A new challenge is then posted on a blank whiteboard, and the process is begun again.

"The Whiteboard Technique is a simple and extremely efficient way to liberate organizational creativity." Bryan adds, "But don't let its simplicity fool you. Many of our clients, including Fortune 500 companies, have achieved extraordinary results with it."

Considering our concept that the office is within you, and the fact that employees may in fact be dispersed in different locations, you might think this idea wouldn't work. But online tools allow you to add a 'whiteboard-like' idea to common software programs, dashboards, or video conferences, as well as in-person. It's one of those magical ideas that connects and empowers across different mediums.

How might you be able to use an idea like this with your team?

Section 4: The Seven Levels of Communication – KNOWLEDGE

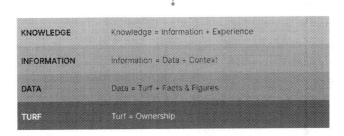

KNOWLEDGE	Knowledge = Information + Experience
INFORMATION	Information = Data + Context
DATA	Data = Turf + Facts & Figures
TURF	Turf = Ownership

Knowledge- "Know-how"—information combined with experience. Experience is seasoned information applied, or knowledge. Because knowledge usually stems from experience, we tend to think of it in terms of the past.

What we know about the past allows us to create belief systems—structured ways of thinking about life, which provide a basis for anticipation of the future.

Be careful of blindly following a belief system simply because it's the only one you've been exposed to. We've done extensive research on the connection of limiting beliefs to generational patterns. These patterns are beliefs that have been passed down from generation to generation, often related to what we think we are capable of or judgments of others. Beliefs that may have protected us in the past but are no longer serving us. Institutionalized, sabotaging beliefs that are prevalent in our culture and may never have been ours. They may have been passed down to us from parents, coaches, teachers, and media.

Communicating in 'knowledge' without awareness of the choice we have in deciding what we believe can be dangerous. What if we took the time to become aware of our beliefs? What if we really challenged and released the ones that aren't true or no longer serving us? What could that mean to you and your potential to communicate powerfully, respectfully, and with greater results? More on this as we travel up the levels but for now be aware of the importance of questioning what you believe to be knowledge. For it may be someone else's truth and not helpful to you or your interactions.

The scientific method is a process used for acquiring knowledge. You ask a question, research the topic, formulate a hypothesis, test the hypothesis with an experiment, then analyze and report your results. You can take the answers from the questions asked in the 'information' chapter and assimilate them into knowledge. This is a powerful way to discover the truth because it is based upon testing and questioning to seek answers over assumptions.

Learning these Seven Levels is just one element of the knowledge you can use as a leader in today's world.

The experience-based system of artificial intelligence is grounded in logic and is making inroads at the knowledge level. The learning element has elevated this data driven system's credibility. Daniela Fazoli says, "Artificial Intelligence and Machine Learning are vast universes and there is so much more out there than we dream possible right now." Just as these technologies are advancing and learning, we as leaders must as well.

The experience of applying information leads to knowledge. For instance, a way to gain knowledge from the past was certain types of books like *The Wonder Book of Knowledge* or the *Encyclopedia Britannica*. But that has all moved into the office of the future and Mind SPACE. All the information you need and found in books can be found at the touch of a button. But is it knowledge without the experience aspect? Not necessarily. It becomes knowledge when you experience the practice or element of a thing. It is integrated into you through familiarity and practical understanding.

Accountability comes into play when communicating in the Knowledge Level. When you have experience of knowledge then you can become accountable for it.

We've all dealt with, and perhaps even worked for, companies with such stringent adherence to procedure that they have taken away the accountability of front-line personnel to do right by a customer. They've removed responsibility and thoughtful custom response in favor of a strict process in the hopes this will increase efficiency. But efficiency must be weighed with service. And service is enhanced when you give the responsibility to your people to recognize, comprehend, and act on the customers' needs.

Communicating from a place of knowledge and accountability enables you to exude and instill confidence.

One story involves an evolved ice cream shop team we met. Each person in this party of customers had forgotten their wallets. Right after ordering, they realized it and told the young man behind the counter to stop scooping. Instantly, he said not to worry. He exclaimed, "Enjoy your ice cream! You can come back to pay." There was no hesitation because he was completely responsible for that decision and confident it was the right one, based on a higher level of service. It was a good business decision because not only did he receive a larger tip when they returned, but he also created loyal customers of that shop.

This level of confidence and ease comes from the knowledge that he is empowered. His manager shared the guidelines of the job but also the underlying values of the company and the experience they wanted for the customer. Then made him accountable for it all while he was working.

- Have you made the transition to apply your experience and information into knowledge?
- Do you as a leader feel accountable for the best results and service?
- Have you empowered your people to be accountable as well?

A Leader's POV: One of the responsibilities of leaders is to know the gaps in what employees know now and what they need to know for peak performance, satisfaction, and growth. To assess and then provide the training and the knowledge to fill the gaps.

Katina Athanasiou fills us in on one silver lining that came from downtime during the pandemic, "The cruise ships have not been sailing and this is the first time we have had the opportunity to cross train across multiple departments. It gives different teams additional insight and knowledge that enables them to do their job better. There's a huge appreciation for that 360-degree view."

This concept of cross training breaks down silos, increases knowledge, and leads to understanding (next up). Cross training can start with something as simple as opening the lines of communication between departments, teams, and roles. Being able to allow for team members to 'try out' the roles is even better because it increases empathy and understanding.

How are you assessing the unique needs of your team?

Section 5: The Seven Levels of Communication – UNDERSTANDING

UNDERSTANDING	Understanding = Knowledge + Empathy
KNOWLEDGE	Knowledge = Information + Experience
INFORMATION	Information = Data + Context
DATA	Data = Turf + Facts & Figures
TURF	Turf = Ownership

Understanding- Connections between people highlight understanding. The word "understanding" is derived from an old English word, "modhoard," which means mind treasure. (You have to do some work to mine the treasure of understanding.)

When we drive in adverse weather (snow, rain, fog) it is easy to lose track of where you are on the road. Looking back, you may see your tracks in the snow, but that doesn't tell you where you are going and what lies ahead. In foggy conditions, your own headlights can confuse you. The same is true in heavy rain. The same can be true when we are trying to understand how to move forward by only looking back.

For instance, many businesses, especially those in the finance area, operate solely on a historic reference model. Approval for a 30-year mortgage requires information about your past ability to pay bills rather than your current or future ability to do so.

Poor weather conditions require you to slow down, be present to what is ahead and around you, and be ready to adapt when conditions change. It's the same for optimal communication that enhances understanding. Become present and focused on the person or team as you interact.

Relationships among people thrive at the understanding level. It is the corporate culture inside the organization, the intricate web so essential for the long-term health of any company.

All too often, a reorganization or the sale or acquisition of large components will rip the finely woven web to shreds. Although the connections of the data and information levels can be made fairly quickly, the re-creation of the corporate culture and outside network at the understanding level is a long and sometimes impossible process without conscious focus on it.

In a discussion on the way we communicate today, we'd be remiss if we didn't discuss communication via social media. As a leader in today's world, becoming aware of your personal brand image as well as the opportunity to connect in this medium with a wider reaching audience must be considered. In order to effectively communicate on social media at the understanding level, it can't be one way. Understanding involves the connections between people.

Looking at how the levels of communication layer on top of each other, you can access the data collected from social media to better understand your customers. For instance, gaining insights from Facebook on your specific audience and how they are engaging (or not!) with you and your company.

Understand the generational element of social media preferences. If you serve Gen Z, you'll skip right over the next part about LinkedIn and instead do more with Instagram, Pinterest, and TikTok (or whatever has cropped up since this printing!). It's worthwhile, because this market uses their preferences not just to engage, but also for commerce and as social consciousness platforms.

LinkedIn if used properly is an excellent tool for business relationship building that leads to better understanding. So, of course, we went to LinkedIn expert and author of *LinkedIn for Personal Branding,* Sandra Long for insights on how leaders are using this platform.

Sandra says, "Many CEOs choose to author articles which will attract candidates, buyers, or partners. Richard Branson writes about the fun workplace culture at Virgin Group. People choose to join companies or buy from those they trust, and this is one additional way to build that authority and connection."

Communicating at the level of understanding requires thought and time. But the results are worth the effort. Using these online tools is an integral part of the mobility of your *office*. We are no longer confined to specific walls to achieve enhanced understanding and rapport. This will require more effort, more ingenuity, and more data-information-knowledge than ever before.

What are some ways that you can increase your communication at the understanding level? Think about this from your perspective. This will be different for everyone. Each person (you, me, your team, or clients) has more facets than the one you see in front of you. During the pandemic we saw so much more of our colleagues, sometimes too much!

Hopefully, we learned that 'Sara', in addition to being an amazingly sharp accountant, also cares for her aging father and has a young child with a disability and a child in Scouts. Our greater understanding of her as a whole person will help us interact with her more fully in our professional setting. We can understand why she is tired, why that last minute request for information was met with silence or why she might react badly at work to something that happened at home. Understanding = empathy.

A few options:

- Create a new habit of a one-minute meditation prior to important calls or meetings to focus you on the present moment.
- Research the person or company you're looking to connect with.
- Survey your employees or clients to learn more about them and their needs.
- Elevate and multiply the connection points; list all the tools available—mail, phone call, social media, email, text, zoom, in-person, etc.
- Enhance your listening skills.

Fill in your own ideas:

-
-
-
-

A Leader's POV: While the capacity for empathy may be innate to some and varies from person to person, it can also be a learned behavior. Understanding it and others better with tools like Emotional Intelligence training can help. Becoming more aware, picking up on verbal and nonverbal cues, and listening with the intention to learn are actions you can take right away to increase understanding and empathy.

One client has a great story about how she consciously moved up the levels from data and information to knowledge and understanding, and how that benefited her company.

Sam is a smart woman in the technology industry with a real knack for numbers and computers. She loves all things tech and often communicates from the space of data and information, sharing graphs, figures, and acronyms that can make your eyes cross if you don't love numbers as much as she does. Sam reached her level of leadership by including moments of excitement about what she learned or created (knowledge).

Working with us, she realized that, in communicating solely from this comfort zone, she was leaving money and relationships on the table. She wondered if her lack of understanding about what her investors wanted has contributed to her company's lack of funding. She started to learn about her connections and what got them as excited as numbers did for her.

She also made a concerted effort to get to know and understand her team better by asking questions about them, their interests, and what they wanted to contribute to the team mission. This helped her hold on to top people through this major transition.

The work she did to understand the priorities of an angel investor enhanced the relationship so much, he decided to give Sam the funding needed to launch a new product. The business exploded as a result.

Understanding the needs of others and becoming present in your conversations to create a deeper connection can have a powerful impact on a leader's business and life.

Section 6: The Seven Levels of Communication – SHARED VISION

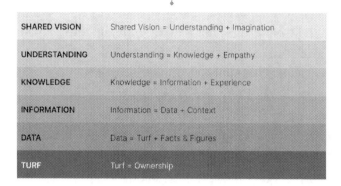

SHARED VISION	Shared Vision = Understanding + Imagination
UNDERSTANDING	Understanding = Knowledge + Empathy
KNOWLEDGE	Knowledge = Information + Experience
INFORMATION	Information = Data + Context
DATA	Data = Turf + Facts & Figures
TURF	Turf = Ownership

Shared Vision- Shared vision includes a call to action that evolves from a keen understanding of what is and what can be, integrating past, present, and future. The axis of shared vision ties Mind SPACE to the Seven Levels of Communication.

President John F. Kennedy had a vision for the United States to send a man to the moon and bring him safely back to earth within a decade. He collected data then put it into context to define what knowledge was needed to make it happen.

Then he determined how that might appeal to the public, asking why was it important to the country to do this?

And from that created a vision the entire country could believe in and support. The vision opened them to what was possible because he used what was important to them in the messaging of it.

Instinctively we know there is a level above understanding that is essential for leadership. The college professor, manager, and scientists can understand their fields and be respected for their wisdom, but that alone is not enough to make them leaders. The truly effective leader thrives at the level of shared vision, a level beyond wisdom.

In the creation of the Seven Levels, revelation of the visionary level came from an interesting source, the culture of the American Plains Indians.

To be recognized as an adult, a young male would go away from the tribe to spend time alone on a mountaintop or in the middle of the plains. During this time of introspection, he would discover the purpose of his own life, made clear in his visions. Upon returning to the tribe, he would be encouraged by his elders to carry out his dream—his life quest. He would come back with a better understanding of his role or how he could best serve the community.

What is Your Life Quest? Your dream, purpose, or mission. What service are you performing for another that is bigger than you?

Does your company have a mission that inspires everyone beyond making a widget or being nice to clients?

What a lesson for us. All too often, people are promoted to management by demonstrating competence of the turf, data, information, knowledge, and understanding levels. Imagine what would happen if a promising person required a visionary quality before being recognized as a leader, even at the first level of management?

The shared vision level includes strategic direction and shared language. This is the level of purpose and excitement. Without the universal commitment that results from a shared vision, organizations eventually lose their direction and zest.

There is a great difference between a shared vision and a strategic plan. Most strategic plans are made up of a lot of data, some information, and a little bit of knowledge. Shared vision, on the other hand, is the communication of the reasons why we do what we do, supported by Data, Information, Knowledge, and Understanding that leads us to our belief in what lies ahead and how we get there. Extraordinary leaders communicate the inward motivation of the Shared Vision as well as the external manifestation of it.

A shared vision typically is articulated by a single person. The words are chosen to inspire the team, the investors, the customers to believe in the vision. The leader doesn't need to be at the top but does need to be in a position to inspire the actions of others. The actions of others are demonstrations of their belief in the shared vision.

Stew Leonard, who created the phenomenally successful Stew Leonard's, 'The World's Largest Dairy Store," has installed a monument at the entrance to his headquarter store with the following vision engraved:

"Rule Number One: The customer is always right.

"Rule Number Two: If the customer is ever wrong, reread rule number one."

His on-target vision of a grocery store as a service business has inspired many other businesspeople to adopt the same philosophy.

What about the shared vision of marriage? Or the lack thereof? Do you know couples who go into this partnership with very distinctly different views of what is and what should be? Even to the extent of how they plan to change not just themselves but also the other person. The absence of a shared vision is what can sometimes cause the breakdown in relationships.

The concept of money, or the bottom line, began as a token of shared trust. According to sociologist William Desmond, "Money was, originally, a symbol for the energy of life, for the power of community and the fulfillment of our deepest human needs... Money is in actuality a symbol of the emotional relations between an individual and other member of the group. It is the record of a complex emotional system comprised of the rights and promises arising out of human actions in the past-and human faith in the future."

Originally, money was a shared vision!

By recognizing shared vision as a strategic resource, we recapture the original meaning of money, which included both economics and human values.

Akio Morita has said that in the early days, when money was scarce, he knew that their "true capital was their knowledge and ingenuity and passion."

To explain how others can create organizational vision, Peg Thoms uses the following exercise in her book, *The Daily Art of Management*.

Imagine that you are Disney. Create a series of 'wouldn't it be great if...' questions. Think about what an ideal park would be like:

- Wouldn't it be great if our park would be appealing to people of all ages, genders, ethnicities, and religions?
- Wouldn't it be great if Disney cartoon characters actually worked at the park?
- Wouldn't it be great if we could charge immense sums of money for admissions and people would pay?
- Wouldn't it be great if visitors could tour the world while in our park in Florida?

The ability to ask the audacious, idealistic questions enable you to work backward to find out just how close you could get.

Do you need to think bigger with your vision?
Do you need to ask different questions?

This big vision is at the core of each of the concepts we discuss. It's the nucleus that holds everything together. It's in the Mind SPACE tool, the Seven Levels of Communication, and scattered throughout as a reminder of the importance of coming together toward a common theme.

Just as a nucleus is "the central and most important part of an object, movement, or group, forming the basis for its activity and growth," the vision of your leadership is the basis for company activity and growth.

We encourage you to find the vision for yourself, your company, your people. Like the office, it stems from within. Focus and passion helps it burn brightly and the vision becomes a guiding light. You, the leaders of the future, have an important role to fill. Change is coming. Change is here to stay. A new level of leadership is required. YOU are the change that is needed to make a real difference in today's world.

The BIG Vision of a "War on Poverty" Required Trust and More- from Will's perspective

After seven years on Polaris, my boss said, "The war on poverty has been declared in Washington and I'd like our company to be involved. And I'd like you to be the one to lead it." I was IN. I had little conversation with the powers that be throughout the process. I just went and did it. Trust is an important component of shared vision. If the vision and the people are strong enough, micromanaging isn't necessary.

The job was to get the folks in Washington to recognize me as a potential school director and to help me. We had a vision of fighting poverty by directly educating young women with potential but lack of means. I met Sister Francetta Barberis, assistant director of the Women's Job Corps, previously president of what was then Webster College. I remember it so well. I was in a room waiting to meet her. She walked in and, at 5' tall, wasn't much taller than me sitting in my chair. Turns out that her vision and ability to build relationships and communicate the vision was what lead to her charming Conrad Hilton, creator of the Hilton chain, into a large donation. This was used to build the Loreto-Hilton Center for the Arts. Sister Francetta was a powerhouse in a small package! She and I became buddies.

When the legislation was passed on the war on poverty there was no funding allocated for facilities. The job corps had the task of finding facilities.

I didn't have much luck finding vacated facilities on the East Coast. Imagine coming into a town in 1965 and telling people that I wanted to bring in a group of disadvantaged young women. I worked my way to the Mid-west and found an old Army Hospital available in Clinton, IA. By this time, I knew I had to work with the media to build a convincing case, along with support from the Chamber of Commerce and the Mayor.

I had two or three quiet meetings and then a larger meeting, and because of the relationships I was building, it was very well received.

Taking the time to build relationships and to create a shared vision for all the stakeholders led to our getting a green light locally and securing a $4.5M three-year federal contract for a great facility to house 600 young women.

Next challenge: Fill the Director of Education position. I found the perfect person the very next day as I watched an interview on public television. Dr. Barbara Mason was principal of Roosevelt Elementary School in New Rochelle, NY. I listened to her speak and said, "That's her!"

The next day I called her and said, "May I have lunch with you?" She said sure, so I flew to New York, and we met. I shared my vision. I told her I had a contract and 65 buildings on 80 acres, "I'm going to build a school for disadvantaged girls, and I need a head of education." Dr. Mason immediately saw the vision. It aligned with her own personal vision. And this is when the magic happens.

The main mission was to educate these girls and get them back out to the workforce. We were excited to get started.

After gathering the hottest educators I could find at the time, I asked them to help me paint the white line down the road... I didn't want a traditional school, but I needed a vision to know where to begin. We went to the blackboard and the lead educator said, "You will not be happy with this." He wrote 'tolerance for ambiguity' on the blackboard.

I didn't realize at the time how important that was, but that's what life is about. To re-reference Robert Jastrow, he said that the 'essence of intelligence is flexible behavior.' That's how we get to where we are and how we evolve.

In building the center, there would be dozens of young women coming to the center every three weeks. The school had to be quite flexible. I couldn't run the school on tolerance for ambiguity alone, so I looked around.

I was reading an article by the head of a community college in Portland Oregon. He said he built the school on the hospital concept. When you arrive at the hospital, they don't do anything until they know exactly what is. Assessing—do you have a broken leg, are you pregnant not pregnant, are you on any medications, many questions. They really understand you before they started the process. And I thought that's my white line down the road! It's a strategy that aligns with the vision.

These kids are going to arrive 16 to 21, female, and that's about the end of the common description. From there anything goes—they could be the mother of three, native Hawaiian, or American Indian, never having experienced dental care but having been a primary caretaker for years. Many different stories. The classes and the environment needed to make sense for them.

Can you imagine a Home Economics class teaching how to cook an egg to a mother who regularly makes meals for three children? It doesn't make sense.

The whole idea was that the school should be flexible enough to really study them for a while and understand their needs. This was important, and Dr. Mason agreed. In this environment, those girls thrived. There was an element of mutual trust. We all worked together toward the shared vision.

My relationships with my bosses had been based on trust and vision. I was free to follow the vision by knowing where they were and discovering the best paths forward. Moving from what IS to what CAN BE. Establishing that trust is one of the foundations of leadership.

It's these elements beyond traditional management strategy and tools that define leadership. Trust. Vision. Individuality. Humanity.

Looking at vision Todd Cherches shares his thoughts on where we have the potential to go. He expresses, "As mentioned above, numbers don't matter... outside of the context in which they exist and the story they tell. So often we get so caught up in the data analytics that we lose sight of the humanity behind the numbers... and start treating people as if they ARE just numbers. In fact, the terms "human resources" and "headcount" reinforce that concept.

"Our humans are not "resources," and they are not just "heads" to be counted. They are individuals with their own personal dreams, goals, and aspirations, and it is only by creating and communicating a shared vision that we can set our people up for success so that they can maximize their performance, their productivity, and their potential."

This ties back to the Understanding level. This layering of skills and focus areas is what contributes to elevated communication.

Todd summarizes, "As Maslow established in his classic "Hierarchy of Needs" model, people need to have their basic human needs of survival and security met, after which they seek a sense of belonging and a feeling of importance. Only then can they aspire to the level of self-actualization. As such, when leadership communicates a strong and compelling vision, people will want to be part of something larger than themselves, as well as contributing their piece of the puzzle to finish off the picture."

- Do you have a vision of how you want to show up as a leader?
- Do you have a vision of what you are looking to accomplish?
- Is it big enough to excite you?
- Do you know how to communicate and share this vision with others?

A Leader's POV: Meeting with Ambassador Melody Garcia, Speaker, PNA Coach, Humanitarian, you can see the passion she has for her why, her bigger vision, and her desire to share the message out into the world with her example.

She reveals, "It is critical for leaders to champion larger causes that impact the world because it is time to start bridging gaps versus the mentality of "staying in your lane". The lesson that the global pandemic truly uncovered is that the world and its leaders cannot continue to think in silos or microscopic focus of just their company, their business, their nation, and their group because everything eventually is interconnected and interdependent.

"We experienced a "global time out" that rendered an equality outside the typical status quo and yet brought about the critical need of socially conscious leaders to truly rise up and communicate in ways that drove in solutions like never before. Prior to the pandemic, humanity had a level of understanding of "connectedness" populated via social media platforms that also disconnected us with the "busyness" of life. Values shifted, including how businesses are operated, and the realization of how dependent we truly are in the survival and success of others in direct relation to our own."

We agree with Melody's assessment that coming from Shared Vision helps leaders, their people, their companies, and beyond. She concludes with, "True leaders never waste a good crisis. It redefines productivity, proficiency, profitability, and performance with focus on value. The value of creativity, of listening from ground up, of collaborations, employee retention, customer satisfaction and being part of a company that not only "meets customer needs" but also pro-actively solves and champions the right behaviors."

Section 7: The Seven Levels of Communication – OUT OF THE BLUE

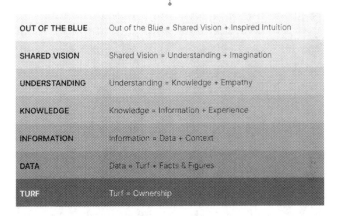

OUT OF THE BLUE	Out of the Blue = Shared Vision + Inspired Intuition
SHARED VISION	Shared Vision = Understanding + Imagination
UNDERSTANDING	Understanding = Knowledge + Empathy
KNOWLEDGE	Knowledge = Information + Experience
INFORMATION	Information = Data + Context
DATA	Data = Turf + Facts & Figures
TURF	Turf = Ownership

Out of the Blue- flashes of insight. Moments of brilliance. As dolphins leap out of the ocean into the sky out of sheer exuberance in being alive, so too do we also experience those moments when life becomes play—and work becomes high play.

Buckminster Fuller said, "The solutions to the world's major problems lie in the imagination." Our dreams, speaking the language of the night in symbols, can solve seemingly unsolvable problems.

Elias Howe, in inventing the lock stitch sewing machine, was stumped by the problem of using a single needle to pick up thread from a bobbin or shuttle on the other side of the fabric. He dreamt that cannibals surrounded him and prepared to cook him as they waved spears. When he awoke, he remembered the spears, which had holes in the shaft and moved up and down.

Albert Einstein described creativity by saying, "I believe in intuition and inspiration. Imagination is more important than knowledge, for knowledge is limited whereas imagination embraces the entire world, stimulating progress, giving birth to evaluation. It is strictly speaking a real factor in scientific research."

We all are born with imagination. Some of us are lucky enough to grow up in a home where we are encouraged to develop our intuition and insight. Then we seek the kind of work where that power is rewarded. How sad it is that so many of us let our insightful curiosity diminish as we grow up. To earn a living, we are often forced by our culture to give up the creative child within us, the quality of the creative child is what the poets, artists, and geniuses are determined to retain.

The out-of-the-blue level of communication provides a vital perspective for leadership. Yet too few organizations encourage thought and discussion at this level.

Too often it is the expert who tries to hold the level of thinking down to his level of knowledge. For example, Lord Kelvin, president of England's Royal Society, is said to have listened to his associates discuss the possibility of flying machines. He didn't directly say they were crazy, but he did cast doubts, insisting that "heavier-than-air flying machines are impossible."

Lord Kelvin was a brilliant scientist, grounded in his thinking, but buried his imagination under the weight of what was known presently, with no room for the future. Eight years after his statement, the Wright Brothers launched their first flight.

We're reminded of the saying that we should give every child two things: roots and wings. Successful managers also need to cultivate both strong roots and wings in their teams.

Some of the most successful businesspeople seem to have a 'sixth sense' in making decisions. Have you ever had a feeling that something was right (or not right) based upon gut instinct that might not have a full rationale to back it up?

The sixth sense was delightfully obvious when conducting a seminar with a group of engineers. A series of exercises allowed them to experience each of the seven levels of communication. They excelled in communication at the data, information, and knowledge levels.

At the understanding level, their excitement grew. So did the significance of what they had to say to each other. When moving to the shared vision and out-of-the-blue levels, they were encouraged to communicate in a way that was totally unfamiliar to them.

Using modeling clay, they were tasked to create a representation of the company Bell Laboratories if it were as good as it could be. They were encouraged to use colors in a meaningful way—green meant okay, red indicated cause for concern, and yellow was somewhere in between. They had fun creating wonderful symbols and images.

On the last day each person was asked to briefly summarize the three days. Everyone spoke of a very positive experience. They were eager to apply what they had learned. However, the last man to speak said he was convinced that he wasn't creative.

He thought that he could not work at the visionary levels and said he was comfortable only at the levels of data, information, and knowledge. Thankful the clay images were kept, his was found and referenced "You are not creative? Look at what you did yesterday."

He had depicted AT&T as a red elephant because he was concerned about the uncertainty caused by the breakup of the Bell System. The elephant's turned up trunk was yellow, indicating his hope that the red condition could change. He had created a green man, wearing a white hat, symbolic of himself, optimistically walking the elephant toward the future, which was represented by a fabulous peacock. He had fashioned the tale of the bird by mobilizing all of the colors together and slicing the clay, showing the beautiful patterns of each feather. His engineering ability was displayed along with his artistic talent.

He said that he wanted to help his client, AT&T, through the transition from being the uncertain red elephant to becoming the proud peacock, which he chose because it represented his vision of the future. He was surprised when told that the tail feather of the peacock is the ancient symbol of hope.

His images and his story revealed a vivid imagination. He did, indeed, wear a white hat. He had forgotten about the skylight of his mind, even denied that quality within himself. All too often, our jobs force us to stay in the lower levels and we forget, even put down our creative ability. Like so many of us, he just needed to be reminded that he does have intuitive and imaginative powers. Leaders have the opportunity to make a major difference in our peoples' lives when we see what they are capable of and help them get in touch with their creative side.

This experience reminded all of us that we have more inside of ourselves than we realize. Psychologist Carl Jung has said that the hands can often solve a riddle the mind cannot.

This man was convinced that he did not have visionary qualities, but doing the playful out-of-the-blue exercise with clay in his hands and forgetting about the facts fooled him into recognizing his creative abilities. He left that meeting with the feeling of being transformed.

In talking about creativity, Jung said, "Fantasy is preeminently the creative activity from which the answers to unanswerable questions come; it is the mother of all possibilities." Fantasy is certainly a wonderful part of the limitless level of out-of-the-blue.

Ingmar Bergman, the Swedish film director, described his creativity in a holistic way when he said, "I make all my decisions on intuition. But then, I must know why I made that decision. I throw a spear into the darkness. That is intuition. Then I must send an army into the darkness to find the spear. That is intellect."

Trust your employees to make the best decisions based upon your vision as well as allowing them to offer creative solutions to problems.

We often experience the biggest blocks in our lives based upon our inability to trust ourselves. We listen blindly to others, trying to make sense of the external noise. Instead, when we quiet that noise and turn up the volume on our heart-centered imagination, we can hear the most important lessons and solutions, as if they are a beacon of light. A light guiding us on which paths to follow.

Have you ever suppressed your natural intuition and then realized you could have avoided a major challenge in your business or life if you had listened? Trust yourself.

Leaders don't always realize that they have the vision for the company as well as their own personal purpose. And when the two are married, greatness occurs. Not everyone knows what their purpose is, so here are a few questions to enlighten the subject.

Helping you unleash imagination, creativity, and intuition. Ask:

- What is the topic that prompts you to talk just a little bit faster or gesture a little bigger or lean forward?
- What do you do extremely well—where is your unique talent?
- What puts you in a state of 'flow' where you completely lose track of time?

Helping you trust yourself and your intuition:

- Make a list of the times you followed (or didn't follow) your intuition. What happened?
- Set mini goals and follow through to completion. Follow-through builds confidence.
- Learn to be comfortable sitting quietly with your thoughts— listening to your inner creativity and intuition for solutions.

Helping you align with company vision:

- What element of the company vision most resonates with you?
- Does it increase your energy and/or elicit solutions?
- How can you offer ideas to move it forward?

A Leader's POV: After reading *Living in a Mindful Universe* by Eben Alexander, MD and Karen Newell, we felt compelled to reach out to Dr. Alexander.

Dr. Alexander was a renowned academic neurosurgeon who experienced a week-long coma that threatened his life and demonstrated powerfully for him a deeper understanding of consciousness, connection, love, and healing.

Within the book he says, "I became aware of a realm that was quite literally outside of the bubble of apparent here and now that is such a staple of our human existence." We get caught up in our thoughts and our focus on self in a way that causes us to forget that we are all interconnected.

Listening to the passion that Dr. Alexander has for this concept of oneness and unconditional love, you can't help but realize the potential that can come from learning from his experience about the responsibility of our choices and the power we have to release ego and lead from truth, compassion, and connection. He talks about the profound power of oneness and how that can be found, not outside of you, but within.

"The human spirit has potential powers far beyond our wildest imagination." He has learned and is sharing all that can come from tapping into this wider consciousness as leaders. His coauthor Karen Newell tells us, "You are the love; it is generated from inside of you. Rather than directing loving thoughts toward yourself, simply be the love that you are."

These concepts tie directly to the Out of the Blue level of communication. Going within to find the universal connection, using it to expand your awareness of what can be, then making better choices in how you innovate, lead, and communicate.

There is hope. Alexander and Newell conclude, "A brilliant, hopeful future is within our grasp – we must simply choose to make it so."

Section 8: The Story

The Avatar

Let's follow client characters through the Seven Levels as they learn and grow. You'll see the process and examples of how each level shows up in the way they are communicating.

As you read through, imagine yourself in each of the levels. Asking questions like the following:

- What level are you in now? How do you know?
- What stories of yours have demonstrated each level?
- Have you found them to be fluid, moving you from one to the other and back again as you develop as a leader?

Joe and Sally have both gone through the challenge of downsizing, each having lost jobs they thought were stable. They are smart, talented professionals in retail. After a time of unsuccessful job search, they realize they are disenchanted with the idea of relying on a company for their livelihood.

Sally, who has been without work for 16 months, shares an idea that's been nagging her at night. She calls her friend Joe, asking him how he feels about starting a consulting firm to provide much needed guidance to companies in transition? While he's never thought of himself as an entrepreneur, Sally's idea sparks his interest.

They talk about it, research options, and agree it would be worth a try. As they start working together, they realize they have very different views of what should happen. They haven't built the trust required for success and so they start communicating in the land of **turf**. Holding back concepts, content, and information in a state of competition and fear. They are hesitant to share their best relationships, which prevents them from being able to market this new company idea.

This level of communicating generates even more fear, anxiety, concern, and challenge. It's a vicious cycle.

Just prior to combusting from the stress, they sit down for a heart-to-heart conversation. They share their concerns and realize their fears aren't based on reality. Opening up helps them understand how alike they are and that they are in tune with where they want to go. This helps them solidify that both really want to make this work. They understand it won't be easy, and communicating in a new way will be most important.

Joe heard about a consultant who comes in and builds bridges to success for partnerships—they are in!

They give all the **data** to Heather. They lay out client names, charts, numbers, product and service lists, everything.

Heather reviews it all and moves them from data to **information** with her pointed questions. Asking, among other questions:

- Why is this idea or service important?
- How will it help clients?
- In what way is it different than others with similar services?

Heather also suggests a focus group with key potential clients to learn what they really need and want. She instructs them on how to use their distinct behavioral styles to communicate more effectively as well as tactics that will help move the business forward. All of this information becomes part of their journey and helps them gain the trusting foundation they require.

The discovery sessions with Joe, Sally, and Heather look at the extensive experience of each. Combine that with the insightful client feedback from the focus group and it gives them the **knowledge** they need to navigate this new business venture. Knowing your client's needs, pain, and goals is a step many new entrepreneurs gloss over.

Sally and Joe grow and learn; they take action, track results, adjust, and change. The business expands. They serve more clients, hire more employees, and on it goes.

As it happens, when you add a layer of process to humans living the human experience it's rarely as linear as one would hope. The new employees do human actions based on human emotions and they slide backward in the levels. The different teams hold fast to their best practices. They become silos of competition and fear of another team stealing their ideas and getting the credit. Yes, they return to **turf**.

But Sally and Joe have been here before. They understand the slippery slope that can take down a partnership, tear apart teams, and dismantle companies.

Their awareness and desire to be better leaders causes them to make changes. They begin holding consistent team meetings to better **understand** the needs of their people. Their goal is to help them succeed, but they need to communicate to understand first.

These meetings help them realize they're missing something. They need to clearly convey what has held them together—their glue. And that's their vision of what is possible. They bring the employees all together at a companywide event to communicate the core values that are the foundation of the company (what is) combined with the vision of what is possible (what can be). This event is a true turning point for their business.

Sharing this vision changes everything for the company. It gives the employees faith in the strength of their company, its leaders, but also something bigger to contribute or aspire to.

What this does for the morale of the organization breaks boundaries of fear. It leads to innovative ideas and open lines of communication as well as thought-provoking strategies, solutions, and significant results.

There is no end to what is possible in this environment. It is filled with **out of the blue** leadership which cultivates the best in their people and company overall!

Anne's Story

Recognize there is nuance in communication and that your goal may not be to move through all the levels, from 1 to 7. It may simply be to become conscious of the levels and move up somewhat depending on the scenario.

The following story is brought to us by communication expert and founder of Speaking Skillfully, Peggy S. Bud. In her words:

Anne is a vice president at a financial institution based in the Washington DC metropolitan area. After reading a blog I posted on LinkedIn, she contacted me to help her with her verbal presentation skills. When she reached out to me, she had been working for the bank for about thirteen years. She had been involved with leadership training through the bank but felt she hadn't gained much from the sessions.

Anne felt her voice wasn't heard and that she wasn't valued as one of the senior members of the team. She was even worried about job security. When she attended senior executive leadership meetings, she was usually the only person in the room with the technical knowledge and sometimes the only woman. She would come prepared with facts and figures, as other team members were not familiar with the political, financial, and credit risk implications.

Anne wanted to prove her worth and highlight her skills, so when asked a question, she would give a tremendous amount of detail, which I refer to as a "verbal dump." In sales they might call it, 'throwing up on the customer.' Telling them everything you know, rather than telling them what they need to know. This often causes people to stop listening and to undervalue the person because it is hard to know or remember the important information. Sometimes her supervisor would ask her 'What are you trying to get at?'

Note from the authors—Anne started with all the 'data' and was communicating it with a great deal of 'information' while trying to insert her 'knowledge.' She wasn't taking into account the end user—the person she was communicating WITH. Anne was missing the important connection of understanding... let's see what happens. Back to Peggy's story.

"Although Anne was more knowledgeable than many of the senior executives, she faced various blocks in being the only woman in the room and the differences in the backgrounds and expertise of her supervisors.

When Anne and I started working together, I helped her learn how to take control of the conversation rather than tell everything all at once. This began with developing strong active listening skills: Listen to the question, restate the question, and then answer the question. Anne learned the value of not sharing all of her knowledge on the topic, but rather answering the questions being asked. She was always prepared to answer follow-up questions. However, in most cases, her initial response was sufficient for the executives in the room, who were not experienced banking professionals.

Anne learned to filter the information she shared at meetings. She divided the information on any given topic into two buckets; the need to know and the nice to know. Usually, the nice to know was not something the senior leaders wanted to hear.

Anne learned the value of communicating from the level of 'understanding' and even dipped her toe into shared vision when looking at the bigger picture of what was needed.

After 6 months of coaching, Anne had an important meeting with some congressional leaders and someone from the Government Oversight Office. At this point, she was implementing strategies, organizing information, and delivering it in small chunks versus her original style of 'verbal dumping.' Because she was prepared, she shared with me that she wasn't nervous or uncomfortable.

The result was the meeting went very smoothly. Anne now understood how to structure the conversation and to take into account the perspective of her listeners. During this particular meeting, she used the approach, 'As a trained banker... and...' which helped her sell herself and her expertise and deliver a clear and memorable message.

Part of being an effective communicator is making sure you deliver the message more than once. After a meeting, Anne started to send follow-up emails to her boss. The email did three things: summarized the key points from the meeting, identified next steps, and made an action statement regarding what she would do next.

Before honing her communication skills, Anne felt that her boss didn't always value what she could bring to the table. After demonstrating improved communication skills, she was asked to attend a very important global meeting. Anne realized the effect of honing and strengthening her communication skills when she overheard her boss say to his boss, "now that's someone you want in your meetings" as she passed them in the hall.

When you use the levels of communication to assess and improve communication, you get results, recognition, rapport, and more.

Will's Process

I used to dream about a musical scale for management communication. Musicians write in a common language, and in another country, even in another century, are clearly understood by other musicians.

In my own management experience, it was difficult to get people, even those who worked next to each other, to understand what should happen next or even what was happening at that moment. We have no common references. (Incidentally, in my later experiences as a corporate officer, the need for common references became even more apparent.) As a program manager, I needed to create order out of chaos.

Moving from the Navy to GE was exciting and challenging. In the Navy, while on the bridge of a ship, I could see the horizon, aided by binoculars, radar, sonar and lookouts. But in GE, where my job was to help create the global support system for the fleet of 41 submarines, I worked in a windowless office. Not only could I not see the horizon, but I also couldn't even see the parking lot.

So I began to imagine a window through which I could see whatever I wanted to see whenever I needed it.

Through the imaginary window of my office a metaphoric ocean began to take shape. It was dark blue at the bottom and grew lighter at the top. I could see **data** piling up at the bottom. At the same time, in my office, I saw boxes of printouts piling up, cheerfully delivered by the data processing people. In desperation I asked them to label the boxes with "graphouts" (summary charts) that would inform me about the contents. Obviously, I needed less data and more **information**.

It was apparent that information, when combined with experience, becomes **knowledge**. In the lighter blue area above knowledge, I was beginning to see the aha level of **understanding** or teamwork, camaraderie, and where other respectful relationships like customer satisfaction abound.

These four levels were adequate for my program management work and served me well as a consultant in later years. But there were levels I hadn't yet discovered.

During a meeting in Washington, DC, Elsa Porter, who was then Assistant Secretary of Commerce, asked why I had stopped at the fourth level. "Why?" I asked. She told me that there were always seven. (This is why mentors and advisors are so important. They unveil things that you may be too close to see.)

I knew there were seven days in the week, seven notes of a musical scale, seven colors of light that are shown through the prism, and even seven wonders of the ancient world. "What are the other three?" I asked. "I don't know," she said, "but you'll find them." The search began.

Clues came from unexpected places. The level of **shared vision** became clear when I read a book about American Indians.

Around the time I was reaching for the level above shared vision, John Naisbitt came to my house to go over his book, *Megatrends*. When that discussion ended, I asked for his advice. I talked about the levels of data, information, knowledge, understanding, and shared vision, and then told John that I could see a white level above the blue where nothing makes sense—it's a place where we use our sixth sense, where we use our other eyes. Out there everything begins with the letter I-insight, imagination, intuition, invention, ingenuity, and even insanity. I said I didn't know what to call it because it's **out of the blue**. John's response was immediate. "Then call it that."

There were now six. What was the seventh? Certainly it wasn't above the limitless level of imagination. Yet, I knew there was another level. And then I realized-It's below data—, the ocean floor which is the earth, or **turf**.

This was the process for how the Seven Levels came to be.

CHAPTER 5

THE NEXT LEVEL

Section 1: Time and Space

We think of ourselves as living in a world where time and space are separate. The truth is our time and space are interrelated; our year is based upon the completion of one orbit of the earth around the sun. The day is one rotation of the earth on its axis. So, time—the year, the day, and even the hour, minute, and second—are concepts related to space.

We envision three offices that can be seen as three ways in which we use our energy, time and space. One is the physical office. The second is the office we hold. The third is the office to which we elect ourselves. We use Past, Present, and Future here but it's not necessarily chronological.

THE OFFICE OF THE PAST –

Data, information, and knowledge are the dominant levels of communication in the physical office, the office of the past. Communication was once limited to the specific place in clock and calendar time; however, with the advent of electronic technology, communication in the physical office is no longer limited in time and space.

"Reach out and touch someone," as everybody knows, is a metaphysical notion. We are encouraged to be in touch without touching. The telephone conversation occurs in metaphysical space. When the telescope, compass, and clock were invented, they were called metaphysical instruments. They performed important functions but no physical work. Beyond physical. Metaphysical.

In the past century, in addition to the telephone, many more metaphysical instruments have been invented—television, computers, recording devices, motion pictures to streaming movie subscriptions, voice and artificial intelligence based virtual assistants—to name the most obvious. A special challenge to management is the effective use of metaphysical space as well as time.

THE OFFICE OF THE PRESENT –

The middle office, designated by the symbol of the organization chart, is the office to which one is chosen—President, C-suite, manager, executive assistant—or in the case of the entrepreneur, the position which the person has created. In discharging the duties of that office, a person can take even greater advantage of the flexibility of space and time.

Space beyond the physical often provides the freedom to work creatively. In this office there is room and time to work at the understanding, shared vision, and out-of-the-blue levels. It is often necessary to schedule a managerial retreat away from the physical office to gain the freedom to work at the visionary level.

Unfortunately, being pulled away from the physical office does not mean that people will always be free to communicate at the higher levels. Too many retreats are clogged with sessions that are steeped in data and information. The skylight of the mind is rarely opened, even though retreats should allow time for creativity. Special time needs to be set aside, even in executive seminars, for exercises in imagination and intuition. But the special time is not just "brainstorming" time. Instead, it is an opportunity to allow and encourage communication at all of the levels.

THE OFFICE OF THE FUTURE –

The power of the third office, the office to which you elect yourself, comes from within. For every individual, this office is truly the office of the future. It is your own self-image. Our own genius, which means individual spirit, gives each of us reason to elect ourselves to an exciting office, recognizing and acting on our own promise and potential.

We can all see ourselves as energy and light. Every atom in our body was once inside a star. We are, in fact, star stuff. There is increasing evidence that atoms within us may have passed through several stars before they became part of us. The human being has been described as a stars' way of looking back at itself. Our brightest people are called stars. When we smile our eyes light up. When we understand, we become enlightened. Even in a cartoon, the bright idea is symbolized by a light.

The strategic resource of the emerging age is a vision that links and motivates people, and the transforming resource is the energy of people that converts the vision into reality. The light of each individual is the essential element of both resources. When we are asked who we are, we usually tell people our job title and the name of the organization that we work for, and yet we know that we are much, much more.

In The Seat of the Soul, the author does a wonderful job of explaining how and why a soul becomes multisensory, moving beyond the traditional five senses. "As a personality becomes multisensory, its intuitions—its hunches and subtle feelings—become important to it. It senses things about itself, other people, and the situations in which it finds itself that it cannot justify on the basis of the information that its five senses can provide. It comes to recognize intentions, and to respond to them rather than to the actions and the words that it encounters."

Author Gary Zukav goes on to explain, "When a multisensory personality looks inside itself, it finds a multitude of different currents. Through experience it learns to distinguish these currents and to identify the emotional, psychological, and physical effects of each. In time, it learns to value and to identify with those currents that generate creativity, healing, and love, and to challenge and release those currents that create negativity, disharmony, and violence."

Becoming aware of the higher energy around us and within us allows for one to lead at a higher level of consciousness.

Section 2: Where is YOUR Office?

Where's the Office? is about opening the minds of top leaders to what is possible. To become intimately aware of the fact that times are changing, and the best leaders don't simply know how to adapt to change, they know how to LEAD it.

We wanted to take you on an adventure, undertaking changes in business as well as the changes in self that are required to best navigate them.

The future of leadership will take place in offices, in homes, and coop workspace. On retreats, at live events, and in virtual meetings. It can be from a phone, a satellite, or an app. Options to gain talent and do work globally has increased. And the most resilient and effective leaders know that it ALL begins by moving YOUR office into your mind by fully utilizing all the skills you have inside of you. Today's office isn't a location, but a mindset. And with an open mind and the right tools, you can succeed.

- Where do you want to work?
- Where will you be most effective?
- How can you support those you lead to consciously choose the office of the mind?

What did you receive?

- The concept of the Office being a 'service done for another'
- The need to move from physical space to Mind SPACE
- Why flexibility in leadership is important in today's world
- How to use the Mind SPACE tool to discover where you are and where you want to go
- The role enhanced communication has in this new environment

- The Seven Levels of Communication tool
- Examples of how leaders are using these tools to succeed today
- A focus on asking the right questions
- An understanding that the office of the future, optimizing the mind, transcends time and space
- Look for the "Keepers" sheet at the end and the link to join a community of other leaders looking to make change and affect major results.

Filling the Gap

Go back to the Mind SPACE tool and look at where you had any yellow or red dots. What notes did you make about where you are? What did you envision for where you want to be?

It's time to do the work and fill the gap between the two.

CHOOSE ONE FOCUS AREA:

Review what you wrote for What IS and What CAN BE:

Make a List of What Needs to Take Place to Move You/Your Team to What CAN BE?

Asking:

- What skills need to be learned?
- What questions need to be asked?
- Who can help me get there?
- What's missing?
- What level of communication (from the Seven Levels) will I need to fill this gap?
- What's the most important thing I can do right now?

NOTES:

- Are you becoming more aware of beliefs or judgments that may be blocking you and your success as a leader? Do you know how to release your attachment to those that limit you?
- Have you taken time to get quiet with yourself and listen to what bigger purpose is igniting the fire within you?
- Do you become present in each interaction, entering relationships with the intention to listen and serve?
- Does your 'office' (performing a service for another) capitalize on your unique gifts and your ability to embrace the idea of fully using Mind SPACE over being tied to physical space?
- Are you conscious of the energy that extends beyond you and how you can use it to lead beyond what you thought was possible?

Section 3: A Call to Action

There is that place of balance where you dive so deep within you that you find the inspired thought that expands beyond you. To an idea that can make a real difference for your team, your company, your community, or the world.

It may be a quiet voice that appears to come from outside of you, taunting you at 3am or distracting you from a mundane task at hand. You find it gets louder when you're alone or quiet. You overcome the fear of it to listen. Just a little. Think about it just a little. Is it possible?

You may be one of the special ones (some call them crazy) who quiet distractions on purpose with the intention of hearing more.

You are intrigued. You know comfortable is overrated. You want something more. You want to make a difference.

People who make a difference go above and beyond. They research the idea. They talk to others who can help make it happen. They do something. They action it. And that's how amazing ideas turn into life-saving products, innovative services, huge contributions to the world. Yes. We want you to embrace your inner crazy. The energy you get from following a bigger purpose will light you up from the inside. Our companies need that energy.

Follow the voice. Take it seriously, because coming from purpose and living a life of meaning is very serious. And possible. And it may seem crazy. You may be called one of the crazy ones. But that's okay, isn't it?

What did Steve Jobs say? "Here's to the crazy ones, the misfits, the rebels, the troublemakers, the round pegs in the square holes ...the ones who see things differently—they're not fond of rules, and they have no respect for the status quo. ...you can quote them, disagree with them, glorify, or vilify them, but the only thing you can't do is ignore them because they change things. ...they push the human race forward, and while some may see them as the crazy ones, we see genius, because the people who are crazy enough to think that they can change the world, are the ones who do." Leaders who cultivate the big ideas in themselves and in others are the ones who make things happen.

The biggest question asked from workshop attendees is, "I have no idea what my purpose is. I want that 'more' but I don't hear it. What if you don't know?!"

First and foremost, if you don't know, recognize that you are not alone. Contrary to this feeling that everyone else has it figured out or that you're the only one who doesn't know… the truth is that most people don't know. They ignored the quiet voice to the degree that they don't even remember ever hearing it. Or they haven't heard it yet.

You're a leader. And if you don't yet know your purpose, it's alright. You can figure it out. You get to choose. We know that choices can change. There is power in this concept that we can choose our purpose for right now, and as our priorities rearrange, our focus clarifies, or certain goals are accomplished, you can make a new decision.

For now, we want to leave you with this:

1. You are not alone.
2. You have a purpose, whether you know it or not, and you can uncover or choose it.
3. Adding meaning to your life doesn't have to be grand.
4. Trust is a part of this. Trust your voice. Don't back away from who you were meant to be.
5. Don't be afraid to try. Even if things don't work out the way you want, you will find a lesson—the lesson imperative to the next level of YOU.

Trust us, regret is way worse than failure. Any time. Any day.

A quick note about #3. Until you find conviction in your purpose, your path, your mission, find meaning in small moments of embracing who you really are. Do good. Show up fully, looking to serve others. And in that, you will be living a meaningful life.

Thoughts?

What is YOUR Shared Vision?

When you lead from the *Shared Vision* and *Out of the Blue* levels of communication, what is driving you? What do you see? How can you connect with it deeply and communicate it so clearly that you inspire people around you to take action toward it?

We understand that this book may have planted the seed for you. And also that life happens. We may get inspired by a new concept, but true change requires more than inspiration. It involves commitment.

Transformation involves going beyond a change in perception to consciously choosing new habits and patterns. And often the fastest path to it is by including reinforcement and accountability.

That's why it was important for us to give you additional tools to encourage and guide you in your journey. Please visit https://bit.ly/wherestheoffice to receive access to resources and connection with like-minded leaders. Look for the following free gifts. The *Conversation with the Authors* video and an additional color *workbook* for you and your team.

We love hearing from our readers. You are always welcome to reach out directly with your questions and success stories.

What the world needs right now is a new kind of leader.

One who has a vision and isn't afraid to share it.

One who is open enough to see and fill the gap in their own leadership style.

And one who is willing to lead from a new location…

The Office of the Mind.

Section 4: Keepers

- People want the freedom to choose where and how they work.
- A leader's openness to change and grow inspires that in others.
- Today's office isn't a location, but is instead, a mindset.
- Many factors play a role in deciding where people do their work.
  - Type of work
  - Need for teamwork and collaboration
  - Cost effectiveness of remote work
  - Desire of employee
- Ability and tools to communicate effectively in that environment
- A leader's ability to access their own intuition, intention, and purpose enables them to see and share a bigger, more engaging vision
- Remote work opens doors to a more global and diverse workforce
- This global perspective requires elevated communication tools to remain truly inclusive and effective
- Think expansiveness over control- trust over micromanagement
- Lifetime security and corporate promises of 30-year careers have been replaced with the security of better mental and physical health and wellbeing
- Choice and personalization have replaced overriding complacency
- Look at where you are and where you want to go- examine the gap
- Bridge the gap with Mind SPACE & The Seven Levels of Communication
- The office of the mind is one that comes from service
- When we realize and set the example that 'the office' resides within us, we foster self-leadership in our people to take

responsibility for their productivity, their mindset, and their performance
- You can connect with openness to any age, sex, race, religion, education, or nationality…as humans having a human experience.
- Movement generates energy that magnifies action and opportunity
- If we as leaders can learn to be forward focused, to be agile in our pursuit of goals, our teams and companies will reflect that as well
- Recognize the unique contributions of each individual
- Growth is the process by which people become connected and human aspirations and organizational results can become one
- Employees want flexibility, well-being, diversity, upskilling, great leadership, and a sense of purpose.
- Release assumptions and ask better questions
- You can and should have a vision of the future but breaking it down into shorter more adaptable plans with built in tracking to assess and tweak as necessary is imperative
- Empathy and authenticity are being embraced as the strengths they are
- As leaders, we must know the impact our actions and our companies have on our clients, community, and the world keeping us focused on the right path and help ensure a sustainable future
- Choice is the balm to change
- The best leaders are those who manage their own mindset, emotions, and behaviors
- A systematic way to define, measure, and improve the quality of communication in the workplace is needed. What we can measure can be replicated
- Communication can improve or reduce efficiency, morale, negotiations, production, and nearly every aspect of business, depending on how well you do it

- In times of change, it is better to overcommunicate, even if it is "we don't know yet."
- Communication is as simple as ABC- start with C!
  - C is your customer or the person who is on the receiving end (conceive the proposition)
  - A is your product or message and how the user needs it (strategize the proposition)
  - B is the delivery system between A and C (dramatize the proposition)
- Mind SPACE is a tool that addresses Shared Vision, Personality, Access, Connection, and Emotion
- Shared Vision- Envision a future of possibility. It applies in any area of business and life, providing clarity, hope, and something to strive for
- Personality- When you move beyond the role a person plays on a team or in an organization and into the fullness of their individual attributes, you can see the possibilities, the potential for each person to excel, but also how fostering that enhances the diversity in ideas, solutions, and collaborative excellence
- A diverse and inclusive organization creates a more productive work environment that not only has better solutions and potential, but also enables development of opportunities for all employees without the fear of judgment and discrimination
- Access- being able to find the resources, tools, equipment, ideas, and skills required to thrive
- Connection- healthy connections in a company lead to more honesty and trust. Ideas and information are exchanged more freely, and this increased flow of productivity and positive energy can have a direct impact on the bottom line
- Barriers to connection can be internal, as in growing self-doubt and fear that we can't reach out to others, or external, as in corporate blocks to keep a traditional organizational structure

- Emotion- emotion is synonymous with mental energy. Understand and harness your emotions for increased creativity
- Turf- teams working on the same project in silos as if it's a "who can get to the answer first" philosophy instead of a process of "if we worked together, we'd all get to a better place more effectively and efficiently"
- Data- includes both useful and irrelevant or redundant information and must be processed to be meaningful
- Information- is data in formation—data in context form, imposed upon unrelated facts and figures
- Use questions to turn data into information- Try the White Board Idea
- Knowledge- applied information and experience lead to knowledge
- Become conscious of the beliefs that guide you and where they came from. You get to choose
- Understanding- spend the time to get present, gain insight, and empathize for better understanding
- Shared Vision- includes a call to action that evolves from a keen understanding of what is and what can be, integrating past, present, and future
- Find the vision for yourself, your company, your people. Like the office, it stems from within. Focus and passion helps it burn brightly and the vision becomes a guiding light
- It's the elements beyond traditional management strategy and tools that define leadership. Trust. Vision. Individuality. Humanity
- Out of the Blue- insight, intuition, imagination, and inspired curiosity that leads to making a meaningful difference- life and business transformation
- Embrace your natural intuition to unleash creativity
- When you use the levels of communication to assess and improve communication, you get results, recognition, rapport, and more

- The power of the office of the future is that it is the office to which you elect yourself. It comes from within
- Become aware of the higher energy around and within you which allows for one to lead at a higher level of consciousness
- Times are changing, and the best leaders don't simply know how to adapt to change, they know how to LEAD it
- There is that place of balance where you dive so deep within you that you find the inspired thought that expands beyond you
- Leaders can sometimes feel alone. Join our community to gain additional resources, accountability, and connection with a powerful network. Go here: https://bit.ly/wherestheoffice

Performance Profile
Mind SPACE

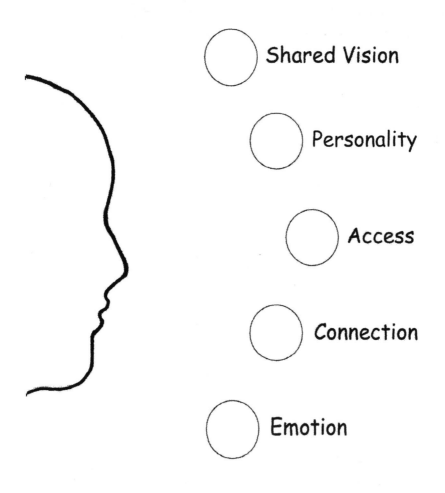

Shared Vision

Personality

Access

Connection

Emotion

ABOUT THE AUTHORS

Wilfred A. Lewis created the visual support system for the deployment of the Polaris Submarine Weapon System and later served as General Manager of GE's advertising agency. Over 50 years ago, he conceived of the concept of moving from physical space to mind space. A visionary ahead of his time. Why pay attention to Will Lewis? He asks key questions and teaches the answers. Where's the Office? is the latest question and you will enjoy the implications of the answer, including the fact that flexible behavior is the essence of intelligence.

Heather Hansen O'Neill is an international speaker, author of Find Your Fire and Teams on Fire!, 2x TEDx speaker, and behavioral expert. She recognized that her friend Will's Mind SPACE idea would be highly relevant in today's world, with those recently forced from their physical space by the COVID-19 pandemic. Heather's mission is to open leader's minds and hearts to the possibility within them.

Question from the author's: See if you can find the clue to our message hidden in the cover. Send your ideas here on LinkedIn and if correct, you'll get a gift: https://www.linkedin.com/in/heatherhansenoneill/

Printed in the United States
by Baker & Taylor Publisher Services